# THE BOUNTY
# MUTINY

Titles in the
## *Famous Court Cases That Became Movies*
series

### The *Amistad* Mutiny
*From the Court Case
to the Movie*
ISBN-13: 978-0-7660-3054-1
ISBN-10:     0-7660-3054-7

### Presidential Power on Trial
*From Watergate to*
All the President's Men
ISBN-13: 978-0-7660-3058-9
ISBN-10:     0-7660-3058-X

### The *Bounty* Mutiny
*From the Court Case
to the Movie*
ISBN-13: 978-0-7660-3128-9
ISBN-10:     0-7660-3128-4

### Racism on Trial
*From the Medgar Evers
Murder Case to*
Ghosts of Mississippi
ISBN-13: 978-0-7660-3059-6
ISBN-10:     0-7660-3059-8

### Evolution on Trial
*From the*
Scopes *"Monkey" Case
to* Inherit the Wind
ISBN-13: 978-0-7660-3056-5
ISBN-10:     0-7660-3056-3

### The Right to Counsel
*From* Gideon *v.* Wainwright
*to* Gideon's Trumpet
ISBN-13: 978-0-7660-3057-2
ISBN-10:     0-7660-3057-1

### Witchcraft on Trial
*From the Salem Witch Hunts
to* The Crucible
ISBN-13: 978-0-7660-3055-8
ISBN-10:     0-7660-3055-5

# THE *BOUNTY* MUTINY

From the
**Court Case**
to the
**Movie**

Edward Willett

**Enslow Publishers, Inc.**
40 Industrial Road
Box 398
Berkeley Heights, NJ 07922
USA

http://www.enslow.com

**Library of Congress Cataloging-in-Publication Data**

Willett, Edward, 1959–
    The Bounty mutiny : from the court case to the movie / Edward Willett.
        p. cm. — (Famous court cases that became movies)
    Includes bibliographical references and index.
    Summary: "Examines the Bounty mutiny and subsequent trials of its participants,
        including the mutineers' plans, the journey of the ship, the trial of the mutineers,
        and the movie made about the story"—Provided by publisher.
    ISBN-13: 978-0-7660-3128-9
    ISBN-10: 0-7660-3128-4
        1. Bligh, William, 1754–1817—Trials, litigation, etc.—Juvenile literature.
    2. Christian, Fletcher, 1764–1793—Trials, litigation, etc.—Juvenile literature.
    3. Bounty Mutiny, 1789—Juvenile literature.  4. Bounty (Ship)—Juvenile
    literature.  5. Mutiny—Oceania—History—18th century—Juvenile literature.
    6. Oceania—Description and travel—Juvenile literature.  7. Pitcairn Island—
    History—18th century—Juvenile literature.  I. Title.
    KF223.B45W55 2010
    910.4'5—dc22

                                        2008044580

Printed in the United States of America

10 9 8 7 6 5 4 3 2 1

**To Our Readers:**
We have done our best to make sure all Internet Addresses in this book were active and
appropriate when we went to press. However, the author and the publisher have no
control over and assume no liability for the material available on those Internet sites or
on other Web sites they may link to. Any comments or suggestions can be sent by e-mail
to comments@enslow.com or to the address on the back cover.

♻ Enslow Publishers, Inc., is committed to printing our books on recycled paper. The
paper in every book contains 10% to 30% post-consumer waste (PCW). The cover
board on the outside of each book contains 100% PCW. Our goal is to do our part to help
young people and the environment too!

**Illustration Credits:** Dixson Galleries, State Library of New South Wales, p. 56; Dixson
Library, State Library of New South Wales, pp. 99, 102; Everett Collection, pp. 3, 15, 43,
68, 90, 107, 109, 112; National Maritime Museum, Greenwich, London, pp. 6, 21, 28, 34,
51, 81; Photos.com, p. 59.

**Cover Illustrations:** Gavel—Digital Stock; courthouse logo—Artville; movie still from *The
Bounty*— Everett Collection.

# CONTENTS

HMS *Duke*, site of the court-martial of the *Bounty* mutineers

# Introduction

*Boom!*

The single cannon shot from HMS *Duke* rang out over the choppy gray water of England's Portsmouth Harbor. It was 8:00 A.M. on Wednesday, September 12, 1792, and the *Duke* had just hoisted a flag indicating that a court-martial was in process.

Thirty minutes later, ten prisoners were led from the gun room of HMS *Hector* and loaded aboard one of the *Hector*'s boats. British Marines stood at attention as the boat's crew dipped their oars and began the journey to the *Duke*, moored in the outer harbor.

More than an hour later, the boat reached the *Duke*. The prisoners were taken aboard and led into the captain's great cabin to face the twelve captains who would serve as their judges and the judge advocate who would run the court. Also present were the prisoners' counselors and various witnesses.

The judge advocate, Captain Moses Greetham, began reading from the circumstantial letter, which laid out the details of the case. The ten men were accused of mutiny, a crime punishable by death.

Specifically, they were accused of the most famous mutiny of all time: the mutiny on His Majesty's Armed Vessel *Bounty*, the ship once commanded by Lieutenant William Bligh.

For more than two centuries, that mutiny has captured the imagination of the world, inspiring histories, plays, novels, at least one stage musical, and five motion pictures.

Oddly enough, it all started with breadfruit.

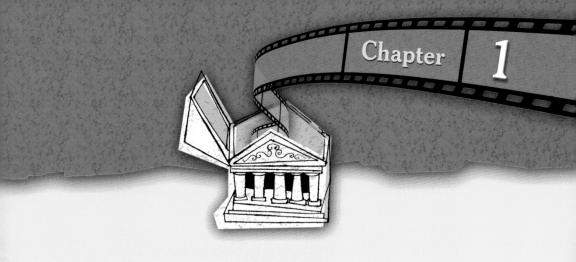

# Chapter 1

# The Voyage of the Bounty

In 1688, while sailing around the world, a naturalist named William Dampier noted an interesting new fruit from the island of Guam:

> The bread-fruit (as we call it) grows on a large tree. . . . When the fruit is ripe it is yellow and soft; and the taste is sweet and pleasant. The natives of this island use it for bread: they gather it when full grown while it is green and hard; then they bake it in an oven . . . the inside is soft, tender, and white.[1]

Later explorers, including Captain James Cook (the first European to visit Hawaii and Australia), also extolled the virtues of the breadfruit. The fruit was so much like bread that some sailors actually preferred it. The bread served on long voyages was a kind of cracker made of flour, water, and salt known as hardtack, or ship's biscuit. Ship's biscuit was so hard it often had to be soaked before it could be eaten. It was also occasionally attacked by wormlike larvae.

As early as 1775 the Society for West India Merchants saw the potential in breadfruit as food for slaves on the British sugar plantations in the Caribbean. The Society offered a monetary reward of a hundred pounds to the first person to bring living breadfruit trees to England.

## A Passion for Botany

Among those with business interests in the West Indies was Joseph Banks. Born in 1743, Banks was independently wealthy and passionately interested in natural history—particularly botany, the study of plants. When he was twenty-one, he collected numerous never-before-seen specimens of plants along the coasts of Labrador and Newfoundland.

He joined Captain James Cook aboard the *Endeavour* when Cook set sail in August 1768 to Tahiti. The ship's visit to Tahiti seized the public's imagination upon the *Endeavour*'s return to England in 1771. Banks had a lot to do with the public's sudden interest. He returned with thousands of specimens, drawings, and paintings.

In 1778 Banks was elected president of the Royal Society, England's top scientific society. For decades very few expeditions of science or exploration were undertaken without his consultation.

Banks wrote and received tens of thousands of letters from all over the world, full of questions and scientific observations. Some urged that the breadfruit tree be imported as a new food source for the West Indies.

Banks could see the fruit's potential. He convinced the British government to mount an official expedition to bring back specimens of the plant.

A former merchant ship called the *Bethia* was purchased and renamed His Majesty's Armed Vessel (HMAV) *Bounty*. The *Bounty* was too small to qualify for the designation His Majesty's Ship (HMS).

Command of the *Bounty* was awarded to Lieutenant William Bligh.

## Enter William Bligh

William Bligh, born September 9, 1754, was the son of Francis Bligh, customs officer at Plymouth, and Jane Pearce, a widow Francis had married ten months earlier.

In 1770 Bligh signed on to the *Hunter* as an able seaman. This was a typical classification for potential officers on ships where all the positions for mid-shipmen—officers in training—were filled. Six months later, a midshipman's position opened up, and Bligh was promoted.

From ages seventeen to twenty, Bligh served as a midshipman on the *Crescent*, sailing to Tenerife and the West Indies. In 1774 he joined the *Ranger*, temporarily reduced to able seaman again, as the ship hunted smugglers in the Irish Sea.

At age twenty-one, Bligh learned that Captain Cook had selected him as sailing master of the *Resolution* for Cook's third expedition. Cook must have heard a good report of Bligh's navigational capabilities. He may also have known of Bligh's talent for drawing. Cook wanted

## Reality vs. the Movie: A Cabin Boy at Age Seven?

Throughout this book, real-life events will be compared to the way they were described or depicted in the 1984 movie *The Bounty*, produced by Dino De Laurentiis. In that movie, Bligh (Anthony Hopkins) tells Fletcher Christian (Mel Gibson) that he has been at sea since he was twelve.

In fact, William Bligh first appears in naval records as a ship's servant on the *Monmouth* at the age of seven—but it is unlikely that he actually went to sea at that age.

In the 1700s Royal Navy captains would often enter youngsters from well-connected families onto the ship's roster, providing them with valuable sea time. Sea time was important because, to become a lieutenant, a young man had to appear on a ship's roster for six years, and he had to serve as a midshipman or master's mate for at least two years of the six.[2] Appearing on a ship's roster at a young age allowed the boy to step straight into a midshipman's position and take his lieutenant's exam sooner.

Bligh probably first went to sea for real at age sixteen, shortly after his mother died.

all his officers to be able to construct charts as well as accurately sketch the various places in which the ship might anchor.[3]

## Sailing With Captain Cook

With Cook, Bligh sailed to Van Diemen's Land (Tasmania), New Zealand, Tahiti, and various Pacific islands. Cook also sailed up the west coast of North America in a failed search for the Northwest Passage (a more direct route from Europe to the Pacific that would avoid the stormy seas around Cape Horn, at the southern tip of South America).

Bligh must have paid close attention to Cook's methods for keeping his crew healthy on long voyages, because he later implemented some of them on the *Bounty*. Second to Cook himself, Bligh was responsible for creating charts and surveys, and he also drew accurate sketches of birds, animals, and landscapes.

On February 14, 1779, at Kealakekua Bay, Hawaii, Bligh witnessed the murder of Captain Cook by natives. In Bligh's view, the murder happened because the Marines guarding Cook did not do their duty.[4] The tragedy affected Bligh not only personally but professionally. Bligh's family connections were just good enough to get him into the Royal Navy as a midshipman, but he had been counting on Cook's influence to help further his career. In the Royal Navy in that era, who you knew was often more important than what you knew.

In February 1781 Bligh married Elizabeth Betham on the Isle of Man. After serving on a variety of ships for a few months, Bligh ended up on the Isle of Man with his wife and new daughter. In the scaled-back peacetime navy, no officers' berths were available.

The peacetime navy paid only two shillings a day, so Bligh had to find other work. The navy granted his request for permission to sail on merchant ships. From mid-1783 until he was appointed commander of the *Bounty*, Bligh commanded ships belonging to his wife's wealthy uncle, Duncan Campbell, carrying goods from England to the West Indies and returning with rum and sugar from the Caribbean.

His careful drawings and proven navigational skills probably recommended him to the Admiralty as commander of Sir Joseph Banks's breadfruit expedition. Navigational skills were important because, once he had retrieved breadfruit from Tahiti, the Admiralty wanted him to chart the Endeavour Straits, a narrow, dangerous passage separating Australia (then called New Holland) and New Guinea.[5] Cook had run aground there.

There is no evidence that Banks ever met Bligh. But Bligh, knowing the career value of a powerful patron, thanked Banks profusely for command of the *Bounty* and wrote: "I can only assure you I shall endeavour, and I hope succeed, in deserving such a trust. . . ."[6]

## HMAV *Bounty*

The *Bounty* was a three-masted merchant vessel, built just two and a half years earlier. She was eighty-five feet, one and a half inches long on the upper deck and twenty-four feet, four inches wide. At just 220 tons, she was much smaller than any of Cook's ships had been.

Because she was so small, she was rated as a cutter. That mattered because a cutter did not have a captain

A breadfruit tree. Many people saw business possibilities in importing the sweet, nutritious fruit to Europe.

or commander as a commanding officer—only a lieutenant. That meant Bligh would not be getting a promotion as he had hoped.

On a voyage expected to last at least two years, the difference between a lieutenant's and commander's pay was considerable. Bligh would earn just seventy pounds a year. As a merchant captain under Duncan Campbell, he had been earning five hundred pounds. All the navy offered was the assurance that he would be promoted upon his return.[7]

The *Bounty* was unusual, thanks to modifications Joseph Banks had insisted upon. All that mattered to Banks was the return of breadfruit and, he wrote, "the Master & Crew of her must not think it a grievance to give up the best part of her accommodations for that purpose."[8]

The most notable modification from Bligh's point of view must have been the loss of the great cabin, the commanding officer's private quarters. Normally, the great cabin was as wide as the ship and extended from the stern almost to the main mast, with windows on three sides providing plenty of light. But on the *Bounty*, the great cabin had been turned into a breadfruit nursery. It was filled with shelves, which were cut with holes to receive 629 pots. It had special ventilation, a stove for warmth, a drainage system that caught and recycled excess water, and more. Bligh had to make do with a windowless cabin, eight by seven feet. He would eat in a small, cramped pantry.

The *Bounty*'s small size meant a smallish crew. Bligh would be the only commissioned officer. Warrant officers would include a master, boatswain, carpenter, gunner, and surgeon. Bligh decided not to hire a purser, who normally bought provisions from the Navy Board, tracked and doled them out on the voyage, and sold back unused ones at the end. Instead, Bligh would look after the disbursement of stores himself.

Most fatefully, the ship would not carry any Marines, who on most Royal Navy ships served as the captain's security and police force.

## The Officers

On August 16 Bligh began appointing his warrant officers. John Fryer would be master and would sleep in the small cabin opposite Bligh's. Fryer's brother-in-law, Robert Tinkler, joined the crew as an able seaman. Although listed as seventeen, Tinkler was in fact only twelve years old.

Thomas Huggan was appointed surgeon. Bligh soon realized Huggan was an alcoholic, and he tried to get rid of him. The Admiralty would not allow that, but it did appoint an assistant surgeon, Thomas Denman Ledward, entered on the roll as an able seaman.

Thomas Hayward, nineteen, had been recommended by a colleague of Banks. He had already served at sea for five years, and although he entered as an able seaman, he would soon be promoted to midshipman.

Other crew members also came aboard. Only two of them had been pressed, or forced into service, which was an unusually low number for the time. Some of the crew members, including both of the pressed men, promptly deserted. As a result, when the *Bounty* finally sailed, she had an all-volunteer crew.

The boatswain, responsible for continually inspecting and repairing all sails, rigging, and boats, was William Cole. James Morrison was the boatswain's mate, who, among other things, administered all floggings.

William Peckover was the *Bounty*'s gunner. Because he had sailed on all three of Cook's voyages, he had already sailed with Bligh at least once. William Purcell, the carpenter, rounded out the warrant officers.

Joseph Coleman, the armorer, had also sailed with Cook and Bligh, as had David Nelson, the botanist whom Banks had appointed gardener. Banks also selected the assistant gardener, William Brown, who had been a midshipman before taking up gardening.

Several members of the crew had sailed on Duncan Campbell's ships, including Lawrence Lebogue, sail

## Pressed Into Service

Under the law of the time, the state had a legal right to the services of all mariners in wartime. Press gangs would roam seaside towns looking for seamen to force into the navy.

Most men who were pressed into service "volunteered" to remain, which earned them the same bonus, and two months' wages in advance, that true volunteers received.[9]

However, many of those pressed into service, and not a few volunteers, deserted almost immediately.

maker; John Norton, quartermaster; Thomas Ellison, able seaman; and the master's mate, Fletcher Christian.

## Mr. Christian

Fletcher Christian was twenty-one years old when he first met William Bligh. About five feet eight inches tall, Christian had dark hair and was strong and well-built. Although generally cheerful and amusing, he occasionally fell into brief periods of deep depression. One officer called him "a tall commanding figure, well adapted to feats of strength and agility. . . ."[10]

Born on the Isle of Man, Fletcher was the son of a lawyer. His family had no tradition of naval service. Nevertheless, at the relatively late age of eighteen, he decided to join the navy. After two years, he, like Bligh, ended up without a berth when the navy downsized.

Christian told a relative that "it was very easy to make one's self beloved and respected on board a ship; one had only to be always ready to obey one's superior officers, and to be kind to the common men."[11]

Through family connections, Christian learned that William Bligh, sailing master for the famous Captain Cook, had just taken command of one of Duncan Campbell's new merchant vessels, the *Britannia*. Bligh received a letter from a Captain Taubman, a friend of his and especially of his wife's family, recommending Christian. Bligh replied that unfortunately he already had a full complement of officers.

Christian then took the unusual step of writing to Bligh directly, offering to sign on as an ordinary crewman until a vacancy opened up. "We midshipmen are gentlemen, we never pull at a rope," he wrote.

"I should even be glad to go one voyage in that situation, for there may be occasions when officers may be called upon to do the duties of a common man."[12]

Bligh, apparently impressed by Christian's attitude, welcomed him aboard on those terms. Christian sailed twice to the West Indies under Bligh aboard the *Britannia*, once as a gunner and once as second mate.

The first mate, Edward Lamb, resented the close relationship Christian enjoyed with Bligh. "You were blind to his faults and had him to dine and sup every other day in the cabin, and treated him like a brother," Lamb wrote to Bligh years later.[13]

Bligh specifically recommended that the Admiralty assign Christian one of the midshipman's posts aboard the *Bounty*, with the understanding that, on his return, Christian could expect to be promoted to lieutenant: the same rank Bligh still held at the start of the voyage.[14]

## Other Young Gentlemen

Several other young gentlemen also joined the *Bounty*. The second midshipman after Thomas Hayward was John Hallett, fifteen, the son of an architect.

Among those enrolled as able seamen, with the understanding that they were in line to become midshipmen if positions opened up, were Peter Heywood, Edward Young, and George Stewart.

Heywood, born in 1772, had served aboard the *Powerful* in 1786, when he was just fourteen. However, the *Powerful* never left harbor, so the *Bounty* would give him his first real sea experience. He was recommended to Bligh by Bligh's father-in-law, Richard Betham, a friend of the Heywood family. Heywood, who had just

© National Maritime Museum, Greenwich, London

**An engraving of Portsmouth, England, the
busy port from which the *Bounty* sailed**

turned fifteen that summer, stayed with the Blighs while the *Bounty* was being equipped.

George Stewart was twenty-one. Bligh had met him through his parents seven years earlier. The last young gentleman, Edward Young, was also twenty-one.

On October 9, 1787, filled with supplies, newly sheathed in copper, and carrying larger-than-usual boats, the *Bounty* sailed up the Thames toward Spithead, Portsmouth. There Bligh would await official orders to sail.

## A Slow Start

After a week at Long Reach pier, near the town of Dartford, where the ship loaded powder for its tiny assortment of guns, plus muskets and bayonets, the *Bounty* proceeded to Spithead. Contrary winds and bad weather turned what should have been a short voyage down the river and around the coast into a three-week struggle. Already it was very late in the season to set sail with any hope of making it through the dangerous seas south of Cape Horn, on the southern tip of South America. But anxious though he was to depart, Bligh could not go anywhere without his sailing orders.

Apparently a mission to collect breadfruit from Tahiti did not rate as high in the Admiralty's eyes as the looming possibility of war with Holland. Three more weeks went by before Bligh received his orders.

Finally, on November 28, 1787, the *Bounty* headed out to sea, but she made it only as far as the Isle of Wight. Bad weather forced Bligh to anchor for the next twenty-four days. The *Bounty* did not head out again until December 23, and promptly found herself in heavy

# Life in the Royal Navy

Everyone in the all-volunteer crew of the *Bounty* knew, in general, what to expect on the voyage.

There would be a great deal of very hard work, sometimes in blazing heat, sometimes in bitter cold; sometimes in the dark or in rain, sleet, or snow; sometimes while massive waves pounded across the deck and threatened to carry off anything and anyone not lashed down.

Under naval regulations, men could be publicly flogged for refusing orders, falling asleep on watch, being too drunk to work, or failing to keep themselves and their clothes clean. After the flogging, the men were expected to simply return to work.

Food was nourishing, if monotonous. It tended to get worse late in a long voyage unless there had been an opportunity to bring fresh supplies on board. There was always plenty to drink, though: Sailors were allowed eight pints of beer a day and a serving of grog—rum mixed with water.

Medical knowledge was poor and the surgeons responsible for applying it sometimes worse. Disease claimed many lives. Any injury requiring major surgery was likely to be fatal because of the risk of infection.[15]

To modern ears, life in the Royal Navy may sound horrible, but it also provided three meals a day and a steady income, plus a chance for travel and adventure. That made naval life more attractive to many men than the sometimes just-as-dreadful life on shore.

weather that almost killed a sailor and carried away some of the ship's extra sails and a yard. It was not until December 29 that the wind fell away to a moderate gale.

On January 5 the ship reached Tenerife, the largest of the Canary Islands off the northwest coast of Africa, and by daybreak of January 6 had moored off Santa Cruz, the largest town. Bligh sent Christian ashore to ask the governor for permission to restock supplies and repair the damage caused by the storm. On January 11 the *Bounty* sailed again.

Like Captain Cook, Bligh took the unusual step of assigning his small crew to three watches, instead of two. That allowed each crewman eight hours of unbroken sleep a day, instead of the usual pattern of four hours on duty, four hours off.

Because they were heading toward the ever-treacherous waters around Cape Horn, Bligh also told the crew he was cutting their daily ration of ship's biscuit by a third so that it would last as long as possible.

## A Clean Ship

Bligh had learned an almost fanatical concern for hygiene from Captain Cook, who lost very few men to disease on his epic voyages. Hoping to emulate him, Bligh followed some of the same procedures, including washing the ship regularly and rinsing it down with vinegar, inspecting the men's clothing, and even checking fingernails every Sunday for cleanliness.

Bligh's concern for his men's health also extended to their diet. Not only did he attempt to procure fresh produce whenever possible, he also made sauerkraut and sweet wort (malt extract) part of the standard rations to prevent scurvy, a disease caused by lack of vitamin C. Bligh's surgeon should have been his ally in all of this. Unfortunately, as Bligh had realized even before he sailed, Thomas Huggan was "a Drunken Sot."[16]

## Across the Equator

It got hotter and hotter as the *Bounty* sailed south, until on February 8 the ship crossed the equator.

Shortly afterward the *Bounty* ran across a whaler called the *British Queen*, bound for the Cape of Good Hope, at the southern tip of Africa. Bligh sent letters home by her, telling both Duncan Campbell and Joseph

## Reality vs. the Movie: The Court of King Neptune

Royal Navy tradition prescribed a humiliating ritual for any sailor crossing the equator for the first time. On the *Bounty*, twenty-seven men were covered with tar, "shaved" with the edge of an iron hoop, and required to give "King Neptune" (one of the old hands) gifts of rum.

The usual ceremony also involved being plunged beneath the water for a terrifying few minutes, but Bligh instituted the gifts of rum in place of the ducking, calling the custom "brutal and inhuman."[17] However, in the movie *The Bounty*, the ceremony proceeds as usual, complete with the ducking Bligh actually forbade.

Banks how pleased he was that he had not yet had to punish a single member of the crew.[18]

A few days later the *Bounty* passed out of the tropics, and temperatures began to drop. On Sunday, March 2, Bligh made Fletcher Christian acting lieutenant and second in command, an indication of how pleased he was with Christian's service. The announcement should have ensured Christian's promotion when the ship returned to England.

A week later Bligh regretfully noted in his log, "Untill this Afternoon I had hopes I could have performed the Voyage without punishment to any One, but I found it necessary to punish Matthew Quintal with 2 dozen lashes for Insolence and Contempt."[19] The punishment would have been carried out by boatswain's mate James Morrison, with Quintal stripped to the waist, spread-eagled, and strapped by the wrists and ankles to a piece of deck grating stood on end.

On March 20 the *Bounty* ran into a storm as she approached the northwesternmost part of the Falkland Islands, forcing Bligh to scrap his plan to stop for wood and water.

Gales came and went. A snowstorm blanketed the ship with snow and ice. Bligh wrote in his log that the conditions were the worst he had ever seen—but things grew worse still. The *Bounty* lost ground as the storms pushed her north. Crewmen began to fall ill and suffer injuries.

Bligh did everything he could to help his hard-working crew. He ordered two men from each watch to supervise the fire and help dry out the others' clothes and hammocks. He made sure there was hot soup for all and hot breakfasts of boiled wheat and sugar. He gave up his cabin to men needing a dry place to sleep.

But on April 17, with the *Bounty* pretty much where she had been twenty-five days earlier, Bligh abandoned the attempt to round the Horn.

Bligh made Fletcher Christian acting lieutenant and second in command, an indication of how pleased he was with Christian's service.

Before leaving England, he had received permission to take an alternate route if the Horn proved impossible. Now, he announced, the *Bounty* would turn east, sail around the Cape of Good Hope, and make her way to Tahiti across the Pacific. It would add some ten thousand miles to the voyage.

## Rest Stop

The *Bounty* reached Cape Town, South Africa, on May 24. The day after their arrival, Bligh had John Williams flogged for negligence of duty in heaving the lead, a weight at the end of a line with knots in it at regular intervals. It was used to measure the depth of the water as a ship approached land.

During the next thirty-eight days, while the *Bounty* was refurbished and resupplied, Bligh and some of his men wrote home. None of the letters mentioned any complaints with the ship or officers. Bligh expressed pride in having reached Cape Town with his crew intact. "Perhaps a Voyage of five Months which I have now performed without touching at any one place but at Tenarif, has never been accomplished with so few accidents,

© National Maritime Museum, Greenwich, London

A ship in a storm off Cape Horn, the southern tip of South America. Bligh had originally intended to sail around the Horn on his way to Tahiti.

and such health among seamen in a like continuance of bad Weather," he wrote in his official log.[20]

From South Africa, the *Bounty* sailed through more severe weather to Van Deimen's Land (now known as Tasmania), anchoring there seven weeks later. Bligh sent work parties ashore to collect wood and water, wash linen, and explore. On August 23 Bligh faced his first serious incident of insubordination. The carpenter, William Purcell, was cutting wood into pieces longer than they should have been. When Bligh complained, Purcell replied angrily that Bligh had come ashore "on purpose to find fault."[21] Refusing orders and talking back to the captain were grounds for court-martial, but a court-martial would have had to wait until the ship returned to England. Bligh's crew was so small that he could not even afford to imprison the carpenter. And since Purcell was a warrant officer, Bligh was not permitted to flog him. Instead, he simply sent the carpenter back to the ship. When Purcell again refused orders three days later, Bligh ordered that Purcell receive no provisions until he carried out his work.

The punishment worked, but James Morrison later wrote that this was the moment when "were sown seeds of eternal discord between Lieut. Bligh & the Carpenter, and it will be no more than true to say, with all the Officers in general."[22] The officer in charge of the wood-gathering party was Fletcher Christian.

## Disputes

On September 5 the *Bounty* sailed for Tahiti. En route, Bligh began to have trouble with some of his officers. On October 6 Huggan, the surgeon, informed Bligh that able seaman James Valentine, twenty-eight, was dying. Huggan had bled him (drained some blood from his arm, a common treatment at the time). The site of the blood draining had become fatally infected.

Valentine died on October 10, shattering Bligh's hopes for a fatality-free voyage. Over the next few weeks, more men became ill. Huggan diagnosed scurvy, outraging Bligh, who considered scurvy a disgrace to any ship.

On October 9 the sailing master, John Fryer, refused to sign the ship's expense books as he was supposed to do every two months. He sent the books back to Bligh and demanded that Bligh sign a certificate saying Fryer had done nothing wrong so far on the voyage.

Bligh ordered all hands on deck. He read the Articles of War, the regulations governing navy ships, which clearly stated it was the master's duty to inspect and sign the books. Fryer signed, but as he did so, he said, "I sign in obedience to your Orders, but this may be Cancelled hereafter."[23]

On October 24 Bligh discovered his surgeon had been drunk in bed for four days. He ordered the surgeon's cabin cleaned out and all liquor removed.

Finally, on the evening of October 25, 1788, Bligh sighted Tahiti, ten months and twenty-seven thousand sea miles after leaving England. To the tired crew, it looked like paradise.

# Chapter 2

# Tahiti

Canoes thronged around the *Bounty* as the ship approached Tahiti. Men and women swarmed up the sides of the ship, climbed the rigging, and crowded the deck. Bligh wrote: "I was so crowded with the natives . . . I could scarce find my own people."[1]

Bligh finally dropped anchor in Matavai Bay on October 27.

The Tahitians had held Captain Cook in high esteem. Bligh had ordered his men not to talk of Cook's death, but he found that another ship had visited the island earlier and told them of the tragedy. However, David

Nelson, the botanist, introduced Bligh to the islanders as Cook's son. (Whether they believed that to be the literal truth, no one is sure.)

Bligh immediately set about gathering breadfruit. He needed permission from the chiefs in whose lands his crew would be working, especially the most powerful local chief, Tynah, and his wife, Iddeeah. Bligh knew them from his previous visit with Captain Cook.

The *Bounty* had arrived near the start of the western monsoon, a period of bad weather running from November to April. Bligh could not follow his orders and sail west to map the Endeavour Straits until the eastern monsoon began in late April or early May. So instead of staying just a few weeks to gather breadfruit, the *Bounty* would be in Tahiti for at least five months.

## Reality vs. the Movie: Bligh's Lie About Cook

In the movie *The Bounty*, when King Tynah says he has heard a rumor that Cook was killed in Hawaii, Bligh denies it. He then defends that decision to his court-martial.

There is no mention in the movie of Nelson making the claim that Bligh was Cook's son. Instead, Bligh tells the court-martial that he lied to the king because the people of Tahiti believed Cook was immortal. They also believed, he says, that all English captains were more or less related.

## Gathering Breadfruit Begins

Bligh established a camp, commanded by Christian, to serve as a breadfruit nursery. Botanist David Nelson and his assistant, William Brown, would transplant seedlings there, then watch over them until it was time to move them to the *Bounty*. Peter Heywood and four able seamen were also assigned to the camp.

Only those men were allowed to sleep on shore. As a result, the ship soon resembled a floating village as women moved in with the sailors living aboard and carried out their daily tasks on the deck.

Bligh knew he needed to maintain good relations with the islanders. To that end, he issued special orders that said, in part:

> Every person is to study to gain the good will and esteem of the natives; to treat them with all kindness; and not to take from them, by violent means, any thing that they may have stolen. . . . No man is to embezzle, or offer to sale . . . any part of the King's stores, of what nature soever. . . . A proper person or persons will be appointed to regulate trade, and barter with the natives. . . . By this means a regular market will be carried on, and all disputes, which otherwise may happen with the natives will be avoided.[2]

By the end of November about six hundred potted breadfruit plants were in the on-shore nursery. Meanwhile, work continued on the ship. Bligh had the sails brought on shore to be aired and dried. The bottom of the large cutter had been eaten by worms, and it had to be repaired and repainted.

© National Maritime Museum, Greenwich, London

**A painting of Tahiti as it may have looked at the time the *Bounty* arrived, ten months after leaving England**

Discipline problems began to crop up. Matthew Thompson was flogged for insolence and disobeying orders. A rudder was stolen from the tent at the breadfruit camp. Purcell, the carpenter, once again refused an order. Bligh confined him to his cabin.

On December 6 a terrible storm made the *Bounty* pitch and roll violently at anchor. Waves crashing over the ship threatened to poison the potted breadfruit plants with salt water. No Europeans had stayed in Tahiti during the rainy season before, so Bligh had not realized that Matavai Bay was a completely unsuitable winter anchorage.

On shore, the river flooded and the sea rose, threatening the breadfruit nursery. Nelson and Brown dug a trench to try to keep the floodwater away from the plants, and only a few were damaged.

After the storm, Bligh wanted to move the ship and the camp at once, but Nelson thought it better to wait until he could be sure some of the apparently dormant plants were alive and healthy.

A few days after the storm, Huggan, the alcoholic surgeon, died—the second European buried on the island.

Around Christmas, the dormant plants started putting out shoots, and the work of moving the camp began. On Christmas Day, with 774 potted breadfruit plants on board, the *Bounty* followed the launch to a new anchorage in sheltered water. Though brief, the journey was almost disastrous: The launch fell astern, and the sailing master, John Fryer, failed to see that the ship was moving into shallow water. The *Bounty* ran aground on the reef. During the tense hours it took to refloat her, she could have been easily pounded to pieces.

The same day the camp was relocated, Bligh had the cook's assistant, William Muspratt, flogged for neglect of duty. Two days later Robert Lamb, the butcher, was flogged "for suffering his Cleaver to be Stolen."[3]

## Desertion

On January 5, 1789, Bligh faced the most serious trouble thus far, when three men deserted: master-at-arms Charles Churchill, able seaman John Millward, and the recently flogged William Muspratt. They took with them the cutter (the smaller of the ship's two boats), plus weapons and ammunition. Thomas Hayward, mate of the watch, was asleep at the time.

The desertion and theft were discovered at 4:00 A.M. when the watch changed. Bligh was informed at 4:30 A.M. He ordered Hayward confined in irons and went ashore, where he told the Tahitians that he expected the men returned.

## Reality vs. the Movie: Asleep or Complicit?

In the movie *The Bounty*, Thomas Heywood, the fictional character who seems to be a composite of Peter Heywood and Thomas Hayward, knows exactly what the men are up to. He permits them to desert without lifting a finger to stop them, then he lies to Bligh when questioned and only claims to have been asleep.

The Tahitians wondered if he would hold some of them hostage on board ship as Captain Cook had done (Cook had suffered desertions on Tahiti on all three of his expeditions). Bligh said he would not, but unless the men were returned, he would "proceed with such violence as would make them repent it."[4]

On board ship, Bligh made a troubling discovery: A piece of paper in Churchill's sea chest bore the names of three members of the shore party, possibly indicating the desertion was intended to be part of a larger plot.

Bligh wrote in a letter many years later that the list had "Christian, Heywood and several other Names on it." He did not believe Christian could be in any way involved, and said that Christian, "when I showed it to him, laughed as well as myself."[5] But it is interesting that three of those in the shore party, Peter Heywood, William Brown, and Fletcher Christian, would later be among the mutineers.

On January 5, 1789, Bligh faced the most serious trouble thus far, when three men deserted.

During the next three weeks, while he awaited the return of the deserters, Bligh discovered that spare sails he had ordered taken out of storage and aired were mildewed and rotting.

A furious Bligh wrote in his log: "If I had any Officers to supercede the Master and Boatswain, or was capable of doing without them, . . . they should no longer occupy their respective Stations. Scarce any neglect of duty can equal the criminality of this."[6]

When the deserters were found, they surrendered without resistance. Bligh ordered them flogged: twelve lashes for Churchill and twenty-four each for Muspratt and Millward, with the same number of lashes administered again eleven days later.

Actually, Bligh was lenient: Convicted deserters could normally expect one hundred to one hundred fifty lashes. Bligh blamed Thomas Hayward, the officer who had been asleep at his post. He was increasingly dissatisfied with the conduct of all his officers. The desertion, running aground, rotting sails—it all demonstrated shoddy attention to duty.

After the flogging, Bligh lectured his officers, warning them that although they were "at present" exempt from flogging, they were still subject to the Articles of War and might yet face "a severe and well-deserved" punishment for their dereliction of duty.[7]

The second flogging took place on February 2. Two nights later someone cut the cable of the *Bounty*'s forward anchor, which could have allowed the ship to drift onto the reef.

The perpetrator was Wyetooa, the *taio*, or special friend and protector, of Thomas Hayward, who wanted to wreck the ship so his friend would not leave. Wyetooa also said that he would kill Bligh if Bligh had Hayward flogged.[8]

## Preparing for Departure

When the time for the *Bounty*'s long-delayed departure approached, the crew began preparing for more months at sea. As the Tahitians realized the ship would soon be sailing away, thefts increased.

The most serious theft was of the azimuth compass. Tynah located the thief and told Bligh he should execute him, but instead Bligh gave him one hundred lashes. The thief was supposed to remain locked up until the ship departed, but he picked the lock and escaped. That prompted another furious outburst from Bligh about the "neglectfull set" of officers around him: "Verbal orders in the course of a Month were so forgot that they would impudently assert no such thing or directions were given."[9]

On March 27 the long process began of bringing more than a thousand breadfruit plants on board. As news spread that the ship was leaving, hundreds of Tahitians gathered. The men said good-bye to their Tahitian friends, lovers, and in some cases wives.

Finally, on April 5, Bligh said good-bye to Tynah and Iddeeah and had them taken ashore in the cutter. Tynah sent it back to the ship full of coconuts. The crew shouted three cheers across the water, and the *Bounty* sailed away into the gathering dusk.

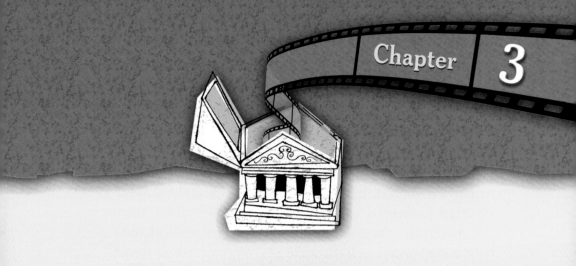

# Chapter 3

# The Mutiny

About a week after leaving Tahiti, the *Bounty* came across an uncharted island called Whytootackee. Shortly thereafter, tensions aboard the ship came to a head.

According to Lawrence Lebogue, the sail maker, soon after the ship left Whytootackee, "[Bligh] came on deck one night and found fault with Christian, because in a squall he had not taken care of the sails."[1]

In his account, the sailing master, John Fryer, said Christian responded with: "Sir your abuse is so bad that I cannot do my Duty with any Pleasure. I have been in hell for weeks with you."[2]

Those are the first words directly attributed to Fletcher Christian in any of the accounts of the voyage. If accurate, they indicate that tensions had been building for a long time.

The *Bounty* next sailed to Anamooka (now known as Tonga), in the Friendly Islands. Bligh, who had been there with Cook in 1777, intended to pick up wood and water. The appearance of the natives who approached the ship appalled him. They looked sickly and bore terrible self-inflicted wounds, part of the local ritual of mourning.

Bligh sent two landing parties ashore. Four men were ordered to gather wood under the command of William Elphinstone. A second party of eleven men under the command of Fletcher Christian would gather water. The wood group had no arms at all. The watering

## The Death of Captain Cook

Bligh probably based his orders to leave the arms ready in the boat on his experience in Hawaii when Cook was killed. After his ship's cutter was stolen, Cook had gone ashore with a party of armed Marines, intending to take a chief hostage. Someone threw something, and Cook fired buckshot from his double-barreled musket. It had no effect. The crowd threw stones, and Cook fired a musket ball from his second barrel, killing a man. Then the Marines fired, but, far from driving the crowd away, it enraged them. They overwhelmed the Englishmen and clubbed Cook to death.

party carried arms, but they were ordered to keep them in the boat.

Bligh knew arms could make a face-off with hostile natives more dangerous, not less. Keeping the arms in the boats ensured that if the landing parties were forced to flee, they would be able to defend the boats that were vital to their escape.

Bligh ordered both parties to have nothing to do with the natives, but the men allowed them to come in close, and an ax and adze were stolen. Bligh was furious. He wrote in his log:

> The cause of this was, that the Officers, contrary to my direct orders, suffered the Indians to croud round them and amuse them. . . . The Men . . . could not comply with every part of their duty and keep their Tools in their Hands, and they therefore merit no punishment. As to the Officers I have no resource, or do I ever feel myself safe in the few instances I trust them.[3]

When natives harassed the watering party, Christian told Bligh he was having trouble fulfilling his duty. According to Morrison's account, Bligh asked "if he [Christian] was afraid of a set of Naked Savages while He had arms; to which Mr. Christian answered 'the Arms are no use while your orders prevent them from being used.'"[4]

Christian and his party were sent back the next day. Later, Fryer went ashore with his own party to speed the task along. He asked a man and woman nearby how to get to the watering place, and they pointed out a path. Fryer met Matthew Quintal rolling a keg of water toward the boat and helped him load it, then they both turned

A movie still from *The Bounty* shows the British ship surrounded by native boats. Bligh knew he had to maintain good relationships with the islanders for the breadfruit project to be successful.

back for the watering place. Fryer met the same couple and gave the woman some trinkets.

Shortly after, Quintal shouted a warning to Fryer that the man was about to hit him with a club. The man escaped, and the unarmed Fryer hurried on to the watering place. He found Christian's party trying to fill the water kegs while surrounded by a group of natives throwing stones. Fryer told Christian to get the casks to the boat, "empty or full," and handed out gifts of nails to distract the crowd.

When the *Bounty* party got back to the cutter, they discovered that the boat's crew had been playing with the children that surrounded the boat, and they had allowed the grapnel, a small anchor, to be stolen off its line by a diver.

Bligh decided he would hold some of the chiefs visiting the ship on board until the anchor was returned. (Cook had held chiefs hostage against the return of stolen items.) Fryer told Bligh the loss was not very great, since there were several grapnels on board, but Bligh responded: "By God Sir if it is not great to you it is great to me."[5]

After the men had a couple of hours to trade for whatever they could get from the islanders, Bligh ordered the *Bounty* unmoored and handed out arms, because he still intended to hold the chiefs for ransom.

Bligh held the chiefs for several hours, but at sundown, although the grapnel had not been returned, he let the chiefs board the canoes that had been following the ship. He gave each of them a hatchet, a saw, and other gifts.

It had been a miserable day for Bligh: Nothing had gone right. The crew probably found his orders to the watering party to leave its muskets in the boat inexplicable, and thinking of their friends on Tahiti, they were probably horrified by his treatment of the chiefs.

## The Infamous Coconuts

From Anamooka, the *Bounty* sailed north toward Tofua. The next day, Bligh came onto the quarterdeck and noticed something odd about his personal stash of coconuts. He called for Fryer.

According to Fryer's account, he said, "Mr. Fryer, don't you think that those coconuts are shrunk since last Night?"[6]

Fryer replied that although they had been stowed up to the rail, they might have been knocked down by people moving around the ship in the night.

Bligh disagreed. Certain that someone had stolen some of his coconuts, he ordered all coconuts brought on deck, along with their owners. Then he interrogated everyone on board.

Morrison said that Christian, when asked how many coconuts he had bought, replied, "I do not know Sir, but I hope you don't think me so mean as to be Guilty of Stealing Yours." To which Bligh replied, "Yes you dam'd Hound I do—You must have stolen them from me or you could give a better account of them—God dam you you Scoundrels you are all thieves alike, and combine with the men to rob me—I suppose you'll steal my Yams next."[7]

As Fryer recounts it, Bligh told the crew he would take care of them for the time being for his own good,

## Reality vs. the Movie: "I Was Thirsty"

In his account of the mutiny, Edward Christian, Fletcher's older brother, wrote that when confronted by Bligh, Christian said, "I was dry, I thought it of no consequence, I took one [coconut] only, and I am sure no one touched another."[8] This is how the event is dramatized in the movie *The Bounty*.

If Christian really said that, it was a shocking example of how lax the officers had become on Tahiti. In the navy, the theft of one coconut was as great as any other theft and demanded swift discipline.

but once he got them through the Endeavour Straits, they could all go to hell.[9] Morrison said Bligh told them he would make half of them jump overboard before they even got through the straits.[10]

He then told the crew that if he did not find out who stole the coconuts, he would reduce their allowance of yams. Morrison also reported that he stopped their ration of grog, and that after Bligh went below, "the officers . . . were heard to murmur much at such treatment, and it was talked among the Men that the Yams would be next seized."[11]

Despite the importance of the coconut incident in the accounts of the mutiny that came later, Bligh did not note the incident in either his personal or public logs.

According to William Purcell, Fletcher Christian felt that if he were to speak up against what he saw as Bligh's unfair treatment, Bligh would break him and possibly even flog him. If he did, "it would be the death of us both, for I am sure I should take him in my arms, and jump overboard with him." Christian added, "In going through Endeavour Straits, I am sure the ship will be a hell."[12]

Ships' captains who flew into towering rages were hardly unknown in the Royal Navy. What seems to have alarmed Christian more than anything else was the notion that Bligh would have him flogged.

That same evening, Bligh invited Christian to dine with him, as had been usual every third evening throughout the voyage. Christian turned down the offer, saying he was indisposed.

## "The People Are Ripe for Anything"

Christian's first inclination after his confrontation with Bligh was desertion, not mutiny. He asked Purcell for some planks, ropes, and nails, then lashed them to the two masts stowed in the launch to make an escape raft. He told several others of his plan, including his friend George Stewart. He also had a hog cooked, which he hid away in a clothes bag with some breadfruit.

But he did not find an opportunity to slip away and eventually went to his bunk, planning to make his move during his 4:00 A.M. watch. Stewart found him there and begged him to reconsider—and quite possibly first put the idea of mutiny into his head.

"When you go, Christian," he said, "the people are ripe for anything."[13]

## Reality vs. the Movie: Around the Horn Again?

In the movie, one of the events that turns the crew against Bligh is his single-minded determination to sail to Jamaica around Cape Horn, both because it is the shortest route and because he is determined to complete his circumnavigation of the world.

In real life, Bligh's orders from the Admiralty were clear: He was to sail through the Endeavour Straits and attempt to map a channel. Bligh would never have dreamed of contravening orders just to gratify a personal desire.

Possibly the filmmakers decided to portray Bligh as determined to sail around the Horn because they had earlier established the Horn's inherent dangers. By contrast, the dangers of the Endeavour Straits, which undoubtedly did contribute to the crew's dissatisfaction, would have required explanation—never as effective as dramatization.

That night, John Fryer had the first watch, 8:00 P.M. to midnight. The weather cleared at about 10:00 P.M. About an hour later, Bligh came on deck. After a brief chat, Bligh went to bed, filled out his log, and went to sleep. He left his door unlatched, as he always did in case he was needed in the middle of the night.

William Peckover took over the watch at midnight. At 4:00 A.M. Christian relieved him.

Christian began sounding out the others on his watch about the possibility of taking the ship. Matthew Quintal said he thought it was a dangerous attempt, and he refused to be part of the plot. Isaac Martin was all for it, and with that support, Christian assembled others.

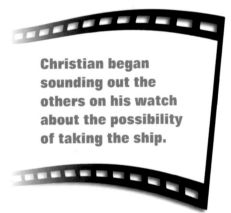

Christian began sounding out the others on his watch about the possibility of taking the ship.

At about 5:00 A.M. Bligh was rudely awakened and hauled out of his bed by Christian, Charles Churchill, John Mills, and Thomas Burkett, all of them armed. More men were outside his door. Shouting "Murder!" and with his hands bound behind his back, Bligh was pushed up onto the deck.

Precisely what happened during the next couple of hours would be the subject of intense scrutiny during the mutiny trials. The bare bones of it, however, seem clear.

Christian intended to put Bligh adrift in the small cutter, but it was so worm-eaten it began to sink the moment it was put in the water. Churchill ordered that the large launch be prepared instead. Twenty-three feet long and six feet nine inches wide at the widest, it was a tiny thing in which to brave the Pacific.

Christian ordered the men he judged loyal to Bligh into the boat. Eventually, including Bligh, there were nineteen aboard, along with supplies: 150 pounds of bread, 32 pounds of pork, six quarts of rum, six bottles of wine, and 28 gallons of water—enough provisions for maybe five days.

While the boat was prepared, Christian held the rope binding Bligh and kept a bayonet pointed at the captain's chest. Bligh wrote later that "he seemed meditating instant destruction on himself and every one."[14]

Hayward and Hallett were among those ordered into the boat. Fryer wanted to remain on the *Bounty* but was also ordered into the launch. Purcell, despite his many disagreements with his captain, elected to join Bligh in the boat. So did others. Those going in the boat tried to gather whatever tools, belongings, and survival equipment they could. Some of those on the *Bounty* tried to stop them, but despite threats and plenty of weapons among the mutineers, the mutiny was bloodless.

## Reality vs. the Movie: The Mutiny

The movie version of *The Bounty* does an excellent job of recreating the confusion that gripped the ship during the mutiny. Men shouting at one another, contradicting, threatening, cursing: It is hard to figure out exactly what's going on, which is one reason that later accounts vary so much in detail.

© National Maritime Museum, Greenwich, London

A painting of the *Bounty* mutiny, showing Bligh and
those loyal to him being set adrift in a tiny boat

Bligh's clerk, John Samuel, managed to retrieve Bligh's log and other important papers. However, years' worth of charts, surveys, and drawings were left behind.

Finally, Christian spoke to Bligh. "Come, Captain Bligh, your Officers and Men are now in the Boat and you must go with them," he said.[15] "If you attempt to make the least resistance, you will be instantly put to death."[16]

Bligh made one last attempt to reason with him. He reminded Christian that he had a wife and four children, "and you have danced my children upon your knee." Christian answered with much emotion, "That,—Captain Bligh,—that is the thing;—I am in hell—I am in hell."[17]

The launch was now overcrowded and overloaded. Some of those left aboard later claimed the only reason they did not join Bligh in the boat was that it looked like suicide. Others loyal to Bligh simply were not permitted to leave; Christian feared he would be left with too small a crew to sail the ship.

Before he boarded the launch, Bligh called out to the loyal members of the crew still on the *Bounty*, "Never fear, my lads, I'll do you justice if ever I reach England."[18]

It took several minutes for the launch to move astern of the *Bounty*, during which time many more shouts, curses, and threats were passed back and forth, along with last-minute provisions. Some of those on the *Bounty* seemed to have suddenly realized the seriousness of what had just happened.

Eventually, Bligh managed to get the oars out, and the launch headed toward Tofua.

And now both Bligh, in the launch, and Christian, commanding the *Bounty*, faced new challenges.

# Chapter 4

# Bligh's Voyage and Christian's Troubles

Bligh wrote in his log shortly after the mutiny:

> I began to reflect on the vicissitude of human affairs . . . but in the midst of all I felt an inward happiness which prevented any depression of my sprits; conscious of my own integrity and anxious solicitude for the good of the service I was on. . . . I began to conceive hopes . . . to be able to account to my King & Country for my misfortune.[1]

By nightfall of the day after the mutiny, the launch had reached Tofua. For three days Bligh scouted along the shore, searching for a good place to land and sending men ashore periodically to look for water, plantains (similar to bananas), and coconuts.

Then some of the island's natives showed up. At first they were friendly, bringing water and trading food for trinkets. But as the days passed, the number of natives increased, and Bligh began to fear an attack. Finally, Bligh ordered his men to gather up their belongings while he continued to trade for breadfruit and spears from the mouth of the cave where they had set up camp.

Then the mood turned ugly. The crowd fell silent, except to knock stones together. "I knew very well," Bligh wrote, "this was the sign of an attack."[2]

The men slowly made their way toward the launch. Two chiefs approached and urged Bligh to spend the night on shore. Bligh replied that he only slept in his boat. The chiefs replied, "Mattie," which, Bligh noted, "directly signifies we will kill you."[3]

Bligh seized one of the chiefs, Nageete, by the hand and, along with Purcell, made his way to the launch. Nageete pulled free as the men scrambled into the launch. John Norton, a quartermaster, jumped into the water to cast off the stern line. The Tofuans threw stones at him and killed him, smashing in his head with stones. Others tried to use the stern line to pull the boat back to shore. Bligh cut it with his knife.

Twelve Tofuans climbed into canoes and chased the launch. Bligh and Peckover threw clothes and other valuables overboard. The Tofuans stopped to retrieve the items, and the launch escaped.

## A Fateful Decision

Their experience on Tofua convinced Bligh and his crew that they could not risk stopping at any more islands. Their only hope lay in sailing thirty-six hundred miles west to Timor, a Dutch settlement where they could find ships to take them back to Europe.

To reach Timor, they would have to go through the Endeavour Straits, the straits Bligh was to have mapped aboard the *Bounty*. They would have to survive on very little food and water—one ounce of bread and a quarter of a pint of water—a half cup—per day.

The crew divided into three watches. One watch would lie on the boards to sleep while the others would bail or work the launch's two sails.

On May 3, the first day at sea, a gale threatened to swamp the boat despite nonstop bailing. Everything they could do without was thrown overboard.

For twenty-four days the men endured heavy rain, gales, and cold nights. Exhausted and starving, some of the men could barely move. To warm themselves, they would dip their clothes into the warm sea, then put them on again wet.

Bligh had no charts, but he did have a quadrant, a compass, a damaged sextant, and the necessary tables for navigation. He made a log line, a rope with knots on it used to measure speed.

Bligh first aimed toward a group of islands the natives of Anamooka had told him about. In the process, he and the crew of the launch became the first Europeans to sail through the islands of Fiji.

Dixson Galleries, State Library of NSW

This painting shows an open boat about the size of that holding Bligh and his men. They had to sail over three thousand miles with little food or equipment to reach safety.

Two weeks after promising to eat only as much as Bligh allowed, some of the men begged him to increase the rations. He refused, even though "our appearances were horrible, and I could look no way but I caught the eye of someone in distress. Extreme hunger was now too evident."[4]

The skies finally cleared on May 23, and the men's spirits were buoyed further by the appearance of birds, a sure sign of nearby land. They managed to capture some of the birds and divided them into eighteen equal parts.

## Landfall in Australia

Bligh knew he must be close to Australia (then called New Holland). He sighted the Great Barrier Reef on May 28 and ranged along it until he found a break through which they could sail into the quiet water beyond. They landed on a small, deserted island.

For two days the exhausted men rested and gorged on oysters and berries. Then they began sailing from island to island along the coast, which Bligh did his best to chart. Eventually, they arrived at the Endeavour Straits, reaching Australia's northernmost point on the afternoon of June 4.

Timor now lay eleven hundred miles away across open water. Their few days of island-hopping had not been nearly enough for them to recover their strength. Now they were once again on short rations.

In the middle of that final stretch, Bligh doubted his men could survive. On June 10 he wrote that their lethargy (they had to be woken up even to receive their meager ration of food), weakness, swollen legs, "hollow and ghastly countenances," and "an apparent debility of understanding, seemed to me the melancholy presages of an approaching dissolution."[5]

Bligh also noted that, according to the boatswain, he "looked worse than anyone in the boat." But he claimed, "I felt neither extreme hunger nor thirst. My allowance contented me, knowing that I could have no more."[6]

Unlike many of his men, Bligh remained alert, continuing to keep his log; make sketches, observations, and soundings; and measure out the rations.

Timor came in sight early on the morning of June 12, but it was not until the morning of June 14 that they found the harbor of Coupang. Two cannons were fired to greet them as they approached. During the journey, Bligh had had a Union Jack made out of scraps of signal flags, and now he hoisted it.

Soon after, the men walked ashore, the stronger supporting the weaker. "Our bodies were nothing but skin and bones, our limbs were full of sores, and we were clothed in rags,"[7] Bligh wrote. But improbably, impossibly, all the men put in the launch—except for John Norton, murdered at Tofua—had survived thirty-six hundred miles in an open boat with what should have been only five days' worth of rations.

Sadly, not all of the survivors would live to see England again. David Nelson, Thomas Hall, Peter Linkletter, William Elphinstone, and Robert Lamb all died in the Dutch East Indies or on the way back to England.

Fletcher Christian, of course, had every reason to think that every one of them had died long since, but he may not have given them much thought at all.

He had his own troubles.

Bligh and his men, thin and starving, are welcomed by the inhabitants of Timor. Remarkably, all but one of the nineteen men put into the launch had survived the arduous journey.

## Aboard the *Bounty*

Immediately after the mutiny, the *Bounty* had no commander. Christian specifically told the men he was not their new captain, that he had no right to command them, and that he would act in any station he was assigned to.[8] However, that was probably just his way of ensuring that he would have their loyalty once he did assume command, which they unanimously urged him to do.

He assigned the necessary duties to various members of the crew and posted an armed guard over the arms chests to ensure that the Bligh loyalists on board did not attempt a counter-mutiny.

After some discussion, the *Bounty* set sail for Tubai, an island about three hundred miles south of Tahiti that Captain Cook had described but had not visited. Christian put the crew into the usual two watches instead of Bligh's three, making for longer shifts, and ordered everyone into uniform to impress the natives they expected to find on Tubai.

The breadfruit plants collected with so much effort on Tahiti were almost all thrown overboard. A few were kept in case breadfruit did not grow on Tubai. The personal possessions of the men aboard the launch were divided by lot.

The *Bounty* reached Tubai one month after the mutiny, at about the same time that Bligh reached Australia. Natives swarmed aboard the ship. The next morning, five Tubaian men escorted eighteen beautiful girls to the ship, and while the sailors were enjoying the girls' company, the men stole everything they could.

Shortly after that, the ship was attacked by fifty canoes manned by spear-carrying warriors.

Christian had expected something of the sort and had loaded the *Bounty*'s small cannon with grapeshot. He fired at the canoes at point-blank range, killing a dozen men and wounding many more.

Despite the confrontation, Christian still thought the mutineers could settle on the island. But a successful settlement needed women, more men, and livestock. In order to get them, the *Bounty* sailed back to Tahiti, arriving on June 6, just as Bligh and his starving men began the final leg of their desperate journey to Timor.

The *Bounty* reached Tubai one month after the mutiny, at about the same time that Bligh reached Australia.

Christian feared the loyalists on board would get ashore and report the mutineers' plans to the next European ship, so he ordered everyone to stay on board. He told the Tahitians that Bligh had met Captain Cook; joined Cook's ship with some of the men, the launch, and most of the breadfruit; and sailed off to found a new settlement in New Holland. He told them Bligh would soon return to Tahiti with more gifts.

The Tahitians gave him more than 460 hogs, fifty goats, chickens, a bull and cow left by Captain Cook a decade before, and even some dogs and cats. Very few natives wanted to come with the crew, though. Only four women—Jenny, Mary, Sarah, and Isabella, who considered themselves the wives of John Adams, Thomas McIntosh, Quintal, and Christian—volunteered, along with seventeen men and boys and one young girl. However, another seven women were tricked into remaining on board.

## Tubai Travails

On June 16, unaware that Bligh and his crew had successfully reached Coupang, Christian sailed back to Tubai. There he and the crew built a fort, cleared land, and planted crops.

Christian maintained rigid discipline. After Matthew Quintal and John Sumner sneaked ashore one night without permission, Christian ordered the mutineers to the quarterdeck, where he put a pistol to Quintal's head and shouted, "I'll let you know who is master." Then he put the men in irons.[9]

It soon became apparent that the colony could not survive. The Tubaians did not want the mutineers there. After the previous bloody encounter, they kept their distance. They believed that a moat around the fort was intended as a mass grave, and they resented the damage done to their crops by the hogs Christian let run free. They also resented the efforts of mutineers to obtain more women from among the local population. Eventually, the Tubaians attacked. Two Englishmen were injured, and sixty-six natives were killed and many more wounded.

By September, uprisings were so constant that Christian could not complete the fort. He saw his control slipping away. He called a meeting, followed by a free vote on what they should do. Sixteen of the twenty-five Englishmen voted to return to Tahiti.

Christian agreed to take them, but he asked that afterward they let him have the ship: "After what I have done I cannot remain at Tahiti. I will live nowhere where I may be apprehended and brought home to be a disgrace to my family."[10]

Eight of the men immediately pledged that they would never leave him.

The mutineers packed up and loaded the great cabin with as many fruit plants and saplings as they could find. They brought aboard the Tahitians and two locals who had become too close to the Englishmen to be safe after they left. They headed back to Tahiti, arriving on September 22, 1789. Midshipmen George Stewart and Peter Heywood, along with Michael Byrne, Joseph Coleman, Charles Norman, and Thomas McIntosh, all set up homes at Matavai. James Morrison, Charles Churchill, Thomas Burkett, John Sumner, John Millward, Henry Hillbrandt, William Muspratt, Thomas Ellison, Richard Skinner, and Matthew Thompson stayed.

Fletcher Christian, Edward Young, John Mills, Matthew Quintal, William McCoy, John Adams, John Williams, Isaac Martin, and William Brown remained with the ship, along with Jenny, Mary, Sarah, Isabella, and the two Tubaians. They hoped to persuade some of the Tahitians to also accompany them.

Christian went ashore briefly for a final word with Stewart and Heywood, urging them to give themselves up if a ship arrived. He asked Heywood to deliver messages to his family and to tell them that he alone was responsible for the mutiny.

He returned to the *Bounty*. Everyone except Stewart and Heywood thought the ship would stay put a couple more days to take on wood and water, but while the twenty-six natives and seven remaining mutineers partied on board, Christian and Young silently cut the anchor rope and sailed the ship out past the reef. One young woman later jumped overboard and swam for shore, but the rest of the natives, taken against their will, sailed away on the *Bounty*.

And that was the last anyone knew of the ship, its crew, and its willing and unwilling passengers for twenty years.

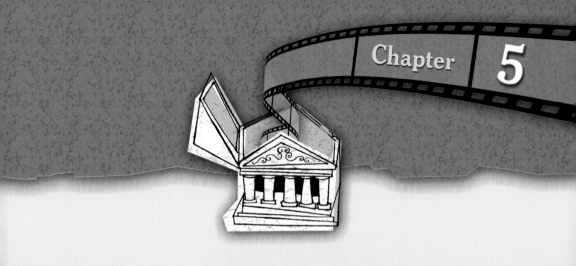

# Chapter 5

# Arrests and Trial

From Coupang, Bligh next had to get his crew to Batavia (present-day Jakarta, capital of Indonesia), on the island of Java, by October. That was when merchant ships would be leaving for Europe, and he wanted his men aboard them.

He purchased a Dutch schooner (using credit from the British government), renamed her the *Resource*, and sailed on August 20, towing the trusty launch.

Bligh had found it hard to arrange the necessary credit to buy the schooner, and he discovered Fryer had told the governor's brother-in-law that Bligh might face serious discipline in England for the loss of his ship.

In his log, Bligh called Fryer "a vicious person," and throughout the voyage to Batavia, Fryer was insolent. At Surabaya, on the coast of Java, he came close to attempting another mutiny. Fryer told Bligh, "You not only use me Ill but every Man in the Vessel and every Man will say the same."[1]

Bligh recounted all the complaints against him in his log—along with the fact that Hayward strongly supported him. He had Purcell and Fryer arrested by the Dutch authorities, then asked any of the other men who had complaints against him to step forward. John Hallett, William Cole, and Thomas Ledward all did so. Their complaints turned out to be minor. Cole suddenly announced that, in fact, he had no particular complaint, and that was the end of the incipient second mutiny.[2]

Ten days after arriving in Batavia, Bligh sold the *Resource* and the launch. The crew dispersed. Bligh arranged for the Dutch authorities to send them home as soon as possible. He put Fryer (released from prison after he wrote an apology to Bligh) in charge, while he, his servant, John Smith, and his clerk, John Samuel, took the first available ship.

Before that ship left, Bligh wrote multiple letters settling accounts and arranging for his men's passage. He also named and described the mutineers and sent out the list to all the ports at which the *Bounty* might turn up.

On October 16, 1789, Bligh sailed for England aboard a Dutch East Indiaman, the *Vlijt*. Put ashore at the Isle of Wight on March 13, he was presented to King George days later.

In June Bligh published an eighty-eight-page written account of his adventures: *A Narrative of the Mutiny, on*

*Board His Majesty's Ship Bounty, and the Subsequent Voyage of Part of the Crew, in the Ship's Boat, From Tofoa, one of the Friendly Islands, to Timor, a Dutch Settlement in the East Indies.*

Bligh's *Narrative*, taken almost directly from his log and the notebook he kept in the launch, caused a stir in London. It even prompted a stage extravaganza, with songs, dancing, and elaborate sets, entitled *The Pirates: Or, The Calamities of Captain Bligh*.[3]

However, for having lost his ship, Bligh was automatically subject to a court-martial, which could not take place until all his surviving crew arrived from Batavia. Of the nineteen men who had been put aboard the *Bounty*'s launch by the mutineers, twelve eventually reached England: Bligh, his clerk, John Samuel, and his servant, John Smith; Thomas Hayward and John Hallett, midshipmen; William Peckover, gunner; Lawrence Lebogue, sail maker; George Simpson, quartermaster's mate; William Cole, boatswain; William Purcell, carpenter; John Fryer, sailing master; and Robert Tinkler, Fryer's young brother-in-law.

Prior to the court-martial, Bligh met with many of the families of the mutineers. All were shocked by their relatives' role in such an inexcusable action.

## Bligh's Court-Martial

The court-martial on the loss of the *Bounty* was held on October 22, 1790, at Spithead, on board the *Royal William*, with Admiral Samuel Barrington presiding. Bligh testified that except for William Purcell (imprisoned in Surabaya), he had no "objection or complaint" against any man or officer. None of the officers had anything to

A movie still from *The Bounty* shows Bligh being taken in his nightclothes by the mutineers. Bligh described the mutiny in a written account of his ordeal.

## Reality vs. the Movie: Bligh's Court-Martial

In the movie, as Bligh recounts events of the mutiny for the court-martial, the movie dramatizes them. His court-martial is presided over by Vice Admiral Lord Hood, and the sharpest questions come from Captain Moses Greetham.

In reality, Admiral Samuel Barrington presided, and the actual operation of the court was delegated to Greetham, judge advocate for both Bligh's court-martial and that of the mutineers.

Also, in the movie, the court-martial happens on land in Wilton House in Wilton, Salisbury, Wiltshire, rather than on board a ship, and only Bligh is questioned. In reality, all the survivors were.

say against anyone else, either. Fryer's testimony agreed with Bligh's that the captain had been bound and held under armed guard by Fletcher Christian.

After deliberation, the court concluded that the *Bounty* was "violently and forcibly taken" from Bligh by Fletcher Christian and "certain other Mutineers." Bligh and all his officers were acquitted except Purcell, who was found guilty in part on six charges and subsequently reprimanded.

After his acquittal, Bligh (thanks in part to the influence of Joseph Banks) was promoted to captain. He soon received orders to sail again to Tahiti and bring back breadfruit. He would be in command of the *Providence*, a three-decked frigate, and be accompanied by the *Assistant*, a four-gun brig. With a larger ship, more officers, and twenty Marines, Bligh sailed in early August 1791.

## The *Pandora*

A month after the court-martial, the Admiralty dispatched the frigate *Pandora*, with a crew of 140 and a strong force of Marines, to search for the missing mutineers. Among those on board: Thomas Hayward, the former *Bounty* midshipman, now a third lieutenant.

The *Pandora*'s commander was Captain Edward Edwards, who had survived his own mutiny nine years earlier (and ruthlessly punished the would-be mutineers, hanging several). The *Pandora* reached Tahiti on March 23, 1791. Before she even anchored, Joseph Coleman, the armorer of the *Bounty*, and several natives came on board.

After his acquittal, Bligh was promoted to captain. He soon received orders to sail again to Tahiti.

Coleman was one of four men who Bligh had stated unequivocally were innocent of mutiny. Coleman told Edwards that two of the sixteen men left on Tahiti by Christian were dead: Charles Churchill, the master-at-arms, had been murdered by Matthew Thompson, who had then been killed by Churchill's Tahitian friends.

Bligh's vouching for Coleman did him no good: He was put in irons. So were Peter Heywood and George Stewart, the next to come to the *Pandora*. Captain

Edwards seemed to have decided that the simplest course of action was to lock up everyone and take them back to England for sorting out.

The Tahitians told Edwards where he could probably find the remaining eleven fugitives. Richard Skinner was brought in on the second day. A party commanded by Thomas Hayward went in search of the rest. Several had settled in a region on the south coast called Papara. Others who had been near Matavai had, just the day before the *Pandora*'s arrival, sailed for Papara in a thirty-foot schooner, the *Resolution*, that they had built themselves.

At Papara, the *Pandora*'s search party found that the mutineers had fled into the mountains, but they soon tracked them down. On Tuesday, March 29, the launch returned to the *Pandora* with James Morrison, Charles Norman, and Thomas Ellison. The *Resolution* was also taken, and Michael Byrne, the *Bounty*'s nearly blind fiddler, either came on board voluntarily or was captured.

The remaining fugitives were caught within ten days: Henry Hilbrandt, Thomas McIntosh, Thomas Burkett, John Millward, John Sumner, and William Muspratt.

## Trapped in *Pandora*'s Box

The fourteen mutineers were placed in a cramped low hut, eleven by eighteen feet, built at the rear of the quarterdeck. They dubbed it *Pandora*'s Box.

Some of the men had Tahitian wives and children; all had the special protectors and friends known as *taio*. The Tahitians wailed and cut themselves in grief, but to no avail: The *Pandora* left Tahiti on May 8, 1791, with the *Resolution* in tow.

For three months the *Pandora* fruitlessly searched island after island for the remaining mutineers. On May 24 five men were lost aboard the yawl, one of the ship's boats, after a four-day storm separated it from the *Pandora*. On June 22 another nine men disappeared aboard the *Resolution*.

The *Pandora* found flotsam from the *Bounty* but nothing else, and in early August Captain Edwards turned for home. At the end of the month the *Pandora* reached the Great Barrier Reef. On August 29, while Edwards searched for an opening, the *Pandora* ran aground—hard. Within five minutes, the water in the hold was four feet deep.

Coleman, McIntosh, and Norman, whom Bligh had named as innocent, were released to help work the pumps. The other prisoners broke free of their irons and begged to be released, but Edwards ordered the irons replaced and the box's entrance bolted shut. As the water rose, the trapped prisoners watched, through the hut's tiny windows, the crew preparing to leave the ship. At the last minute, the armorer's mate, Joseph Hodges, climbed into the box and removed their irons. Muspratt and Skinner, the first freed, and Byrne, who had not been in irons, all escaped. Then someone barred the door again, with Hodges inside the box. He kept working, removing the rest of the irons.

Abruptly, the ship rolled to port, dumping men into the water. Water poured into *Pandora*'s Box. William Moulter, *Pandora*'s boatswain's mate, heard the cries of the men inside it and opened the door. The men fought their way out.

The lifeboats circled the wreckage, rescuing anyone they found. Thirty-one of the ship's company and four prisoners died: Richard Skinner, John Sumner, George Stewart, and Henry Hilbrandt.

## On to Coupang

On August 31 the lifeboats set out on the 1,100-mile journey to Coupang. Although the men suffered terribly from thirst, they had food, and arrived safely at Coupang on September 16.

On October 6 the entire company set sail for Batavia as passengers on a Dutch East Indiaman, the *Rembang*.

The *Rembang* arrived in Semarang, on the north coast of Java, on October 30. There, much to their astonishment, the men of the *Pandora* discovered the mutineers' homemade schooner, the *Resolution*. Her crew had made their way to the Dutch East Indies in the four months since losing sight of the *Pandora* in a storm. The *Rembang* and *Resolution* sailed together to Batavia.

During the next seven weeks in Batavia harbor, most of the prisoners were allowed on deck only twice. Ironically, that may have saved their lives. On shore, fifteen of the *Pandora*'s crew died of illness.

Edwards divided his company among four ships bound for Holland. The ten remaining mutineers all went aboard the *Vreedenburg* with Edwards and another twenty-six men and officers. At the Cape of Good Hope, the mutineers and Edwards transferred to a British ship, the *Gorgon*, where the prisoners were treated much better than Edwards had treated them, and they began to regain their health and strength.

On June 19, 1792, the *Gorgon* arrived in England, anchoring at Spithead off Portsmouth. Two days later the mutineers were sent by longboat to the *Hector* and locked in the gun room. Although dark and airless, the room had canvas-walled cubicles for the prisoners to sleep in. Aside from being shackled in leg irons, the prisoners were well-treated.

## Preparing for the Court-Martial

Convicted mutineers could expect to hang. During the next few months, their families did everything in their power to help them. Most of the mutineers did not have the naval and legal connections necessary for a strong defense. One who did was Peter Heywood.

Heywood's sister, Hester, wrote everyone associated with the *Bounty* she could find. Her uncle, Captain Thomas Pasley, after talking to some of the *Pandora*'s crew, wrote her that "your Brother appears by all Account to be the greatest Culprit of all" except for Christian, and that "on Trial I have no hope of his not being condemned."[4]

Heywood wrote his family while in Batavia. In his letter, Heywood claimed that those who did not wish to remain with Christian had been given the choice of either being taken as prisoners to Tahiti and left there or joining the overcrowded launch.

Heywood claimed he chose to remain on the ship, not realizing that his conduct would be construed as mutinous, "owing to my Youth & unadvised Inexperience."[5] (Heywood was only sixteen at the time of the mutiny.)

Through his family connections, Heywood hired as his legal adviser John Delafons, an authority on courts-martial. On Delafons's advice, Heywood wrote the Admiralty requesting a speedy trial, claiming he wanted his guilt or innocence established as soon as possible. More likely, Delafons wanted to have the court-martial before Bligh could return from his second breadfruit expedition to testify against the mutineers.

Although the court-martial could take place without Bligh, it could not take place until Lord Hood, commander in chief at Portsmouth, returned to port. On August 16 the entire fleet, including Hood's flagship, the *Duke*, anchored at Spithead.

## Judges Selected

Besides Hood, required by law to preside, eleven other judges—all captains—would sit in judgment. Several were from ships that had just returned to Portsmouth with the fleet. Other captains arrived later.

The Admiralty summoned its witnesses (or evidences, as they were called), who included John Fryer, William Cole, William Purcell, William Peckover, John Hallett, and Captain Edwards.

Oddly, Robert Tinkler was not summoned. As Caroline Alexander notes in her book *The Bounty*, "this was fortunate for the Heywoods. The fact that young Tinkler had just turned fourteen at the time he joined Bligh and Fryer in the open boat would have been highly inconvenient to Peter's plea of 'youth and inexperience.'"[6]

Heywood's uncle, Thomas Pasley, in his own questioning of the witnesses, had heard encouraging reports that Heywood had not been an active member of the mutiny. However, he could still be found guilty for not having tried to stop the mutiny.

The Heywood family hired Francis Const, the lawyer of Peter's late father, to represent him. Pasley did not think it was a wise choice. Although Heywood did his best to prepare, he knew he was not ready to answer questions.

Then Aaron Graham, a friend of Pasley's with extensive experience in naval courts, joined Heywood's defense. On September 5 Graham met with Pasley and Const. Afterward, Pasley was much more hopeful. "I have every Reason to think you may look forward with pleasing Hopes," he wrote to Peter.[7] After Peter met Graham himself on September 8, he too felt much more confident.

## Final Preparations

Details of the trial still had to be ironed out. Hood wanted to try the mutineers as a group; they wanted to be tried separately. The court decided to try them as a group.

The location was debated, but in the end it was held on Hood's flagship, the *Duke*, to ensure that the location would not be grounds for later appeal.

The exact charges had to be determined. There was some talk of charging the prisoners with piracy, but the charge was taken from Article XIX of the Articles of War: "If any Person in or belonging to the Fleet shall make or endeavour to make any mutinous Assembly upon any Pretence whatsoever, every Person offending herein, and being convicted thereof by the Sentence of the Court-martial, shall suffer Death."[8]

Though lacking Haywood's connections, the other prisoners had also been preparing as best they could. Morrison and Burkett had letters from officers they had served under previously, testifying to their good character. Only William Muspratt had managed to obtain a lawyer.

On September 12 the ten prisoners were rowed from the *Hector* to the *Duke*. The court convened, and the charges were read. Finally, the accused mutineers told their stories.

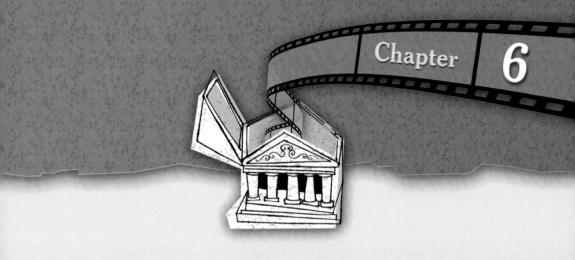

# The Testimony

During the first two days of the trial, Fryer, Cole, Purcell, and Peckover each described the events of the mutiny. Burkett, Muspratt, and Millward were named by Fryer and Cole as having been armed during the mutiny—an offense that would almost surely result in their being hanged. Cole said Heywood intended to come with the loyalists but was kept below decks. He also defended Morrison.

Purcell said that Millward had been forced to take part in the mutiny and that Heywood had been a victim. According to Purcell, Heywood had had a cutlass in his

78

hand, but as soon as Purcell said, "In the name of God, Peter, what do you do with that?" he dropped it. "In my mind he had no hand in the conspiracy," Purcell testified.[1]

On the third day, Hayward and Hallett were called as witnesses. Hayward said he thought Morrison had assisted the mutineers, and he believed Heywood had as well. Hallett said he had seen Morrison armed and jeering at Bligh, and that at one point, Heywood had laughed, turned around, and walked away after Bligh spoke to him. Morrison, Muspratt, and Millward all asked John Smith, Bligh's servant, to verify various aspects of their accounts, but he could not or would not.

It appeared that only the three defendants Bligh had named as loyal—Coleman, McIntosh, and Norman—had unequivocally been so. Of the remaining seven, three—Burkett, Millward, and Ellison—had been described as active mutineers by everyone. Of the remaining prisoners, all except the blind fiddler, Michael Byrne, had been seen armed during the mutiny.

The final witnesses for the prosecution were Captain Edward Edwards of the *Pandora* and his officers. Two days before, Edwards had been acquitted of the loss of the *Pandora* at his own court-martial. Now he confirmed that Coleman had tried to board the *Pandora* even before she anchored and had helped Edwards find the other men. He also confirmed that Heywood, Stewart, and Byrne had also come on board voluntarily.

Joseph Coleman was the first prisoner called to defend himself. After the previous testimony, no one doubted his innocence.

## Peter Heywood's Defense

After that, Peter Heywood began his defense. Thanks to his family connection, his fate was of most interest to the many onlookers crowded into the *Duke*'s great cabin. Heywood stated that he was too weak to defend himself properly and asked the court to permit Const, his second lawyer, to read his statement for him.

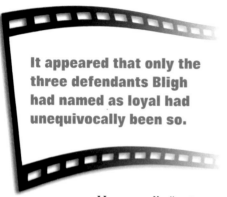

It appeared that only the three defendants Bligh had named as loyal had unequivocally been so.

The statement set forth three lines of defense. First was Heywood's "extreme youth and inexperience." Upon being awakened the night of the mutiny, he claimed, he did not really understand what was going on.

Const read:

> The Boat and Ship . . . presented themselves to me without its once occurring that I was at liberty to choose, much less that the choice I should make would be afterwards deemed Criminal; and I bitterly deplore that my extreme youth and inexperience concurred in torturing me with Apprehensions and prevented me from preferring the former; for, as things have turned out, it would have saved me from the disgrace of appearing before you, as I do at this day.[2]

Second, Heywood claimed the launch was so overloaded by the time he had gathered his wits that it would have been "a kind of an act of suicide" to climb aboard her.[3]

He even claimed he had helped save the men in the launch, because if one more man had gone aboard it,

© National Maritime Museum, Greenwich, London

A portrait of the mutineer Peter Heywood, painted many years after the mutiny. Heywood used his youth and inexperience as a defense at his court-martial.

it either would have sunk or the crew would have had to throw overboard so many provisions they would never have made it to land.

Third, Heywood claimed that after someone on deck told him that if he stayed on the ship he would be deemed guilty of mutiny, he immediately went below to gather up his possessions, but he was held there by Charles Churchill against his will.

Witnesses corroborated Heywood's account (even though parts of it contradicted his own earlier accounts of events). Captain Edwards and Lieutenant Larkan of the *Pandora* confirmed Heywood had come on board voluntarily and had helped Edwards determine what had happened to the *Bounty* after the mutiny.

In the final statement in his defense, Heywood claimed that if Bligh had been present, he would "have exculpated me from the least disrespect."[4] Bligh almost certainly would have done no such thing, but fortunately for Heywood, Bligh was on the other side of the world.

## The Other Defendants

Michael Byrne said he would have gotten into the launch if he had been able to see, but because he could not, he had gotten into the cutter instead. Afterward the mutineers would not let him get into the launch.

Next was James Morrison, who had already impressed the judges with his vigorous cross-examination of witnesses. Like most of the others, Morrison had the judge advocate read his statement. Morrison claimed he had initially hoped to help retake the ship, but when a counter-mutiny failed to materialize, he remained on board because the launch was so overloaded that another man would sink her. He also stated that he had handed into the launch some last-minute supplies and a couple of cutlasses.

In response to Hayward's testimony that Morrison had looked happy rather than unhappy when preparing the launch, Morrison said he had put on that expression to keep himself safe among the mutineers.

Hallett had claimed to have seen Morrison carrying weapons. Morrison denied it. Purcell corroborated his denial. Hallett had also claimed that Morrison had shouted jeeringly after the departing boat, "If my friends enquire after me, tell them I am somewhere in the South Seas."[5]

Unfortunately for Morrison, Cole said he remembered hearing something like that, too. So did Purcell, although he could not say for sure who had said it. Cole, Fryer, and Purcell all said Morrison had been a man of good character.

Charles Norman, whom Bligh had proclaimed innocent, testified he had been ordered by Christian to help prepare the cutter, and he had been aboard her when she was lowered into the water. He discovered her hull was so worm-eaten he could not keep the water out. Back on the ship, he helped Purcell prepare the launch and tried to go aboard her, but Christian ordered him, Coleman, and McIntosh to remain on the *Bounty*.

After Norman came Thomas Ellison, who had claimed to be nineteen when he joined the *Bounty* but was actually Heywood's age.

Like Heywood, Ellison relied on youth as a defense. "I hop[e] your honours will take my Inexpearance'd Youth into Consideration," he wrote. "I never did or me[a]nt any harm to any one. . . . I hope . . . yo[u]'ll be so kind as to take my Case into Consideration as I was No more than between Sixteen and Seventeen Years of age when this was done."[6]

Unfortunately for Ellison, at some point he had grabbed a weapon and shouted that he would stand sentry over Bligh; Christian reprimanded him for it, but the fact remained he had taken up arms.

Thomas McIntosh, also exonerated by Bligh, came next. He recounted how he had been ordered to prepare first the cutter, then the launch, and how he had brought up tools and other items he thought those on the boat might need. He also testified that Christian had ordered Churchill to keep McIntosh, Coleman, and Norman from joining the others in the launch.

William Muspratt, the only defendant besides Heywood with a lawyer, definitely needed one. Hayward and Cole both testified that they had seen Muspratt armed with a musket, and he had been one of the men who had tried to desert at Tahiti.

Muspratt's lawyer first tried to call as witnesses two other prisoners, Byrne and Norman, whose innocence seemed straightforward. He pointed out that this was commonly allowed in criminal courts on land when several people were tried on the same charges. However, it was not commonly allowed in courts-martial, and so the request was denied.

Muspratt claimed he had picked up a musket only to help Fryer attempt to retake the ship, and that the testimony against him from Purcell and Hayward could not be believed because it was self-contradictory.

Thomas Burkett gave a long, detailed defense, even though Bligh had specifically named him as one of those who had dragged him from his bed in the middle of the night. Burkett claimed that Christian had forced him to take part. He swore he would have helped retake the ship if only someone had made the attempt.

Burkett pointed out (and Peckover had already confirmed) that he asked the officers in the boat if there was anything he could get them, and he retrieved some of Peckover's clothes and his pocket book. Burkett also noted that he obtained a compass for the boat, and that he came down from the mountains of Tahiti voluntarily.

The final defendant was John Millward, who had deserted on Tahiti. Fryer had testified that Millward had been armed during the mutiny but nevertheless had seemed friendly. Millward also swore he had been willing to help retake the ship. He said Alexander Smith had put a cutlass into his hand, and he had immediately put it down again. Later, he said, Christian ordered him to take up arms again, and he was afraid to refuse.

## The Verdict

Court was adjourned until nine o'clock the following morning, Tuesday, September 18. The prisoners were asked if they had anything more to say. Peter Heywood did: He provided three attestations to the time and date of his birth to prove that he was as young as he claimed.

The judges cleared the court while they deliberated. At 1:30 A.M. the prisoners gathered in the great cabin, faced the twelve captains, and awaited the verdict.

# Chapter 7

# The Verdict and What Came After

Lord Hood proclaimed the verdict:

> It is agreed that the charges have been proved against the said Peter Heywood, James Morrison, Thomas Ellison, Thomas Burkett, John Millward and William Muspratt, and I do adjudge you and each of you to suffer death by being hanged by the neck onboard such of His Majesty's ship or ships of war, at such Time or Times and at such Place or Places" as should be directed. . . . [I]n consideration of various Circumstances, [the Court did] humbly and most earnestly recommend the said Peter Heywood and James Morrison to His Majesty's Royal Mercy.[1]

Charles Norman, Michael Byrne, Joseph Coleman, and Thomas McIntosh were acquitted.

With that, the court-martial adjourned, and the prisoners were taken back to the *Hector* while Norman, Coleman, McIntosh, and Byrne were immediately released.

Muspratt, through his lawyer, immediately filed a petition protesting the fact that he had not been allowed to call witnesses he believed could have proved his innocence, even though he would have been able to in a court on land.

On October 27 Peter Heywood and James Morrison were summoned onto the *Hector*'s quarterdeck, where Captain Montagu read them the king's unconditional pardon. In a brief prepared statement, Peter Heywood pledged to be faithfully devoted to the king's service in the future.

## Hanged From the Yardarm

The following afternoon, John Millward, Thomas Burkett, and Thomas Ellison—whose youth and inexperience, unlike Heywood's, had not been enough to earn the king's mercy—were taken from the *Hector* to the *Brunswick*, the ship on which the executions would take place. At 9:00 A.M. on Monday, October 29, a gun fired and a yellow flag fluttered up to announce the executions. Boats ringed the *Brunswick*; men, women, and children crowded the shore.

Just before 11:00 A.M. four clergymen led the prisoners up to the fo'c'sle. Bags were placed over their heads and nooses around their necks. The rope leading to each man's noose was assigned to a crew of men. They now pulled hard, as though hoisting a sail.

"Thomas Burkitt was Run up to the Starboard Fore Yard Arm, Milward and Ellison to the Larboard, and There Hung Agreeable to their Sentence," Captain Curtis wrote in his log.[2]

After two hours, the bodies were cut down and taken away to be buried.

Morrison returned to naval service after his acquittal. So did Heywood.

By early December Muspratt learned that his petition had been successful: He had been reprieved. On February 11, 1793, he learned that the king had also pardoned him.

## Bligh's New Expedition

Bligh's new ship, the *Providence*, had sailed with her tender, the *Assistant*, on August 3, 1791. Bligh fell ill at Tenerife with a high fever and headache (probably due to malaria) that made him occasionally issue illogical commands. He relieved himself of command, handing over the *Providence* to Lieutenant Nathaniel Portlock, who had been commanding the *Assistant*, while he went aboard the *Assistant*.

Bligh did not resume full command until after a six-week layover at Table Bay on the Cape of Good Hope. His ships arrived at Tahiti on April 9, 1792. Once again he set about cultivating breadfruit. During his stay he heard stories about the *Bounty*'s brief return trips to Tahiti after the mutiny.

Bligh fell ill again toward the end of June, but the expedition left Tahiti on July 19 carrying 2,126 breadfruit plants. The ships carried on through the Endeavour Straits, which Bligh successfully charted for the Admiralty. After nineteen cautious, painstaking days, Bligh's ships reached the Indian Ocean. They arrived at Coupang on October 2. At Coupang, Bligh would have learned of the shipwreck of the *Pandora* in the waters he had just successfully navigated.

The expedition delivered more than a thousand breadfruit plants to St. Vincent, in the West Indies, on January 23, 1793. Delayed by the outbreak of war between England and France, Bligh did not reach England again until early August. He found that despite his successful voyage, he no longer seemed to be in favor with the Admiralty.

## The Smearing of William Bligh

While Bligh was away, Peter Heywood's relatives had been doing their best to damage Bligh's reputation in naval circles. By making him out as a villain, they made Heywood's actions seem more reasonable. The Christian family, too, anxious to repair their reputation, did their best to blacken Bligh's name.

In November 1792 Peter Heywood (or his lawyers) wrote to Edward Christian expressing the opinion that Fletcher was not

> that vile wretch, void of all gratitude, which the world had the unkindness to think him; but . . . a most worthy character; ruined only by having the misfortune . . . of being a young man of strict honour, and adorned with every virtue; and beloved by all (except one, whose ill report is his greatest praise) who had the pleasure of his acquaintance.[3]

An engraving of Captain William Bligh. Families of the mutineers did their best to smear Bligh's reputation after the court-martial, painting him as a tyrant.

With that letter, which made its way into the newspapers, Heywood recast Bligh as the villain of the mutiny—and provided Edward Christian with the excuse he needed to launch his own public investigation. By the time Bligh returned to England, Edward Christian's investigating committee had been at work for a year.

That committee included, among others, four theologians and two lawyers. Most were abolitionists (people working to abolish the slave trade); the breadfruit plants Bligh had been sent to retrieve were intended primarily to help feed slaves in the West Indies.

Most of the committee had never been to sea, and they did not understand that Bligh's actions and verbal outbursts were hardly unusual in the Royal Navy.[4]

The accounts that seemed so horrifying to Edward Christian's committee had not raised an eyebrow among the sea captains at the court-martial. Some of the men from the *Bounty* defended Bligh against charges of cruelty after Edward's account appeared. "I have heard the Captain damn the people, like many other captains," Lawrence Lebogue stated, "but he was never angry with a man the next minute, and I never heard of their disliking him."[5]

Heywood recast Bligh as the villain of the mutiny—and provided Edward Christian with the excuse he needed to launch his own public investigation.

John Hallett agreed that Bligh could express himself "in warm or hasty language, when the conduct of his officers or people has displeased him; but . . . situations frequently occur in a ship when the most mild officer will be driven, by the circumstances of the moment, to utter expressions which the strict standard of politeness will not warrant."[6]

## Bligh Returns

Edward Christian's report had not yet been published when Bligh returned aboard the *Providence*, but Joseph Banks passed along some of the preliminary papers and notes from the investigation. Bligh said it was "low abuse" that was beneath his notice.

Meanwhile, James Morrison was preparing his own account. His complaints all seemed to center around food: He claimed that the men were shorted while Bligh took the best for himself. But he also claimed that most of the incidents took place on the way to Tahiti, and his claims were contradicted by the letters crew members and officers had sent back from the Cape of Good Hope. Bligh's reaction to Morrison's papers, also passed on to him by Banks, was blunt. "Morrison's accounts are made up of vile falsehoods which no body will dare to publish or sustain," he wrote to Banks.[7]

Morrison was the first to publicly say that Christian originally intended to leave the *Bounty* on a makeshift raft; Bligh thought the claim was ridiculous. Probably due to Banks's influence, Morrison's narrative was never published, but its contents must have been circulated privately.

Bligh was wrong to discount the effect of the two narratives. It took nineteen months for Bligh to receive a new commission. During that same period, Heywood, despite having been found guilty of mutiny, was on his way to a respectable Royal Navy career.

Edward Christian's account of the mutiny appeared toward the end of 1794, as an appendix to a partial transcript of the proceedings of the court-martial. That transcript only included the arguments of the prosecution, with none of the statements from the defenders—some of which would have undercut Christian's version of events.

## Bligh Responds

Bligh responded within a month. The document and affidavits he published included the orders he had written controlling trade with the natives on Tahiti, the deserters' letter of apology, statements taken by the Dutch authorities in Batavia, and statements by some of the same men Edwards had interviewed.

Lebogue, for instance, noted that Edward Christian had asked him whether Bligh flogged his people, why he kept them on short rations, and about how he had behaved aboard the *Providence*. Lebogue had replied, "Captain Bligh was not a person fond of flogging," and added, "some of them deserved hanging, who had only a dozen."[8]

Publicly, Bligh's rebuttal seemed effective. But his straightforward telling of the tale could not compete with the romantic image of Fletcher Christian, the tortured, sensitive soul, forced to take desperate action to overthrow the tyrant who had made his life on board the *Bounty* a living hell.

The version of the story concocted by Edward Christian would grow and blossom in the public consciousness until it completely crowded out the facts.

## The Rest of Bligh's Career

Bligh's career continued to be an eventful one. In April 1795 he was appointed captain of the armored transport *Calcutta*. Then in 1797, while in command of the *Director*, he was involved in another mutiny—but one that involved many ships.

The Nore mutiny was really a labor strike. A few days earlier, sailors at Spithead had gone on strike to demand higher wages, better food, and better care for their sick and wounded. Lord Howe negotiated an end to the strike, giving in to most of the demands.

The sailors at Nore followed suit, with a new set of demands that included the removal of various unpopular officers. Several of the captains who had served at the *Bounty* mutineers' court-martial were among those ordered ashore. William Bligh was not.

When he was finally removed from his command, a week into the mutiny, he defended his crew to the Admiralty, saying that the trouble had started on a different ship. The Admiralty put down the mutiny, hanging, flogging, or transporting (sending off to prison in Australia) the worst offenders. Bligh was one of the captains chosen to go to the seamen and urge them to return to duty. One of the few concessions Howe made was to agree to remove more than a hundred of the most resented officers: again, Bligh's name was not on that list.

Once again in command of the *Director*, Bligh took part in a blockade of the Dutch coast with the North Sea fleet. In October 1797 he fought in the Battle of Camperdown. Following that, he requested a medical leave of absence for a rheumatic complaint.

In 1801, commanding the *Glatton*, Bligh fought in the battle of Copenhagen, receiving a personal commendation from Lord Nelson, then the second in command.

In 1805 Bligh journeyed to New South Wales, in Australia, as governor. In 1808 he was thrown out of office in a coup, and he spent two years imprisoned on a ship off shore. In 1811 Bligh testified at the rebels' court-martial. During the trial he faced hostile questions about how often he had been involved in a mutiny, and how often a court-martial, a clear indication of how the mutiny on the *Bounty* continued to haunt his career.

In 1812 Bligh's wife, Betsy, died, not yet sixty years old. John Fryer died the same year.

## The Fates of the Crew

Robert Tinkler, the youngest member of the crew of the launch, died eight years after Fryer. He had eventually achieved the rank of commander.

Charles Norman died in December 1793. John Hallett, who joined the *Penelope* after the court-martial, died in December 1794 at the age of twenty-two. An obituary noted he had lost the use of his limbs temporarily after the open-boat voyage and before his death had permanently lost the use of them again.

Lawrence Lebogue died in 1795 aboard the *Jason*, moored in Plymouth Harbor. He was forty-eight.

Thomas Hayward, after returning to England with the last of the *Pandora*'s crew in September 1792, joined the *Diomede* and survived another shipwreck when the ship hit a rock off the coast of Ceylon. In 1796, at the age of twenty-nine, he was appointed commander of the *Swift*. It was lost at sea with all hands in a typhoon in the South China Sea.

George Simpson died in his hammock in the *Princess of Orange* in 1801.

William Muspratt avoided the noose, but he did not live much longer than if he had not: He was dead by 1798.

James Morrison eventually achieved the rank of master gunner. In 1806 he was serving aboard the *Blenheim*, which ran onto a sandbar en route to the Cape of Good Hope. The commander managed to get the severely damaged ship to harbor in Madras but then decided to press on to the Cape. The ship vanished with all hands.

The fate of some of the other *Bounty* survivors is not known. Joseph Coleman spent some time in hospitals after the court-martial, then served with Bligh on the *Director* and the *Calcutta*. He entered a hospital ship in November 1796 and does not appear in any records after that.

John Smith remained with Bligh until 1801. McIntosh joined the merchant navy. Nothing else is known about them. Bligh's nephew, Francis Blond, interviewed Michael Byrne during the time Bligh was gathering statements in his defense against the charges by Edward Christian. After that, Byrne vanishes from the records.

In 1803 Peter Heywood achieved the rank of post-captain, and he served until his early retirement in 1816.

In 1817 Vice Admiral William Bligh died while walking along Bond Street on his way to visit his surgeon. He probably had stomach cancer.

Joseph Banks died in 1820. He had worked hard to protect Bligh's reputation. After his death, the story of the tyrannical Captain Bligh gathered fresh steam.

## Peter Heywood's Final Years

Heywood married in 1816, the same year he retired. In 1830 a captain named Edward Belcher paid Heywood a visit. Just three months later, Belcher married Heywood's stepdaughter.

*Bounty* historian Caroline Alexander believes Belcher blackmailed Heywood by threatening to reveal that he had perjured himself at the court-martial. She thinks Belcher knew that, far from being held below, Heywood had been on the gangway and could easily have boarded the launch if he had so wished.[9]

Heywood died on February 10, 1831, at fifty-eight years old.

How could Belcher have known enough about the mutiny to blackmail Heywood? Perhaps because he had spoken to the only other man still living who had taken part in the mutiny: the last survivor of the men who had sailed from Tahiti with Fletcher Christian.

## Life and Death on Pitcairn's Island

In February 1808 an American sealer called the *Topaz* found land that did not exist on charts. The captain, Mayhew Folger, deduced that it must be Pitcairn's Island, discovered forty years earlier but misplaced on the charts by about 180 miles.

Pitcairn's (now just known as Pitcairn) is tiny, two miles long and a mile wide. Forested and surrounded by high cliffs, it was supposed to be uninhabited. As the *Topaz* drew near, three young men in a canoe came out to meet the ship and astonished the crew by speaking English.

Folger soon realized he had discovered the final destination of Fletcher Christian and the *Bounty*. Once on shore, he found about thirty-five people, mostly women, youths, and children—the families of the mutineers. The oldest youth, about eighteen, was named Thursday October Christian. He was the son of Fletcher Christian.

Only one mutineer, Alexander Smith, was still alive. He told Folger the mutineers had run the *Bounty* aground and then set up a settlement. They had prospered at first, although two of the mutineers died in the first two years, one of illness, one by suicide.

A few years after that, six or seven of the survivors, including Fletcher Christian, were killed by the Tahitians. Smith had been wounded but survived. The mutineers' widows had then killed their husbands' murderers, leaving him alone with all the women and their children.

The Admiralty heard all this and ignored it. Six years later, in 1814, when two British naval ships found the island again, the world took notice.

During the next few years, several more ships stopped at Pitcairn Island. To one captain, Alexander Smith revealed his true name: John Adams. He had used an alias when he joined the *Bounty*.

Adams told many different versions of what had happened on Pitcairn Island. He told the captains of

Dixson Galleries, State Library of NSW

Pitcairn Island, the destination of the *Bounty* mutineers. Descendants of the mutineers and Tahitian women live on the tiny island even today.

those first two British ships that Christian had changed after the mutiny and "by many acts of cruelty and inhumanity, brought on himself the hatred and detestation of his companions."[10] He was shot by one of the Tahitians while digging in his field, less than a year after the mutineers landed.

However, in later versions Adams said Christian had gone insane, committed suicide, or simply died of illness.

## Adams's Most Complete Account

In 1825 Captain Frederick Beechey stopped at the island for sixteen days aboard the *Blossom*. Adams gave him one of the most complete accounts. He recounted how the mutineers had burned the *Bounty* once they unloaded her, an event depicted right at the end of the movie *The Bounty*.

The massacre of the mutineers by the Tahitians seemed to have occurred because the mutineers treated them like slaves. To Beechey, Adams once again said that Fletcher Christian was killed while working in his yam field.

Edward Belcher was one of the young officers aboard the *Blossom*. In Belcher's opinion, Beechey did not get as accurate an account as the officers did. In author Caroline Alexander's opinion, it was the account of the mutiny Belcher had heard that day from Adams that gave him the information he needed to blackmail Peter Heywood five years later.

Alexander also believes that one of the main causes of problems on the island was the unhappiness of the women, who, with the exception of those accompanying

▪▪▪▪▪▪▪▪▪▪▪▪▪▪▪▪▪▪▪▪▪▪▪▪▪▪▪▪▪▪▪▪

Fletcher Christian, Matthew Quintal, and Adams, had all been kidnapped.

Teehuteatuaonoa, nicknamed Jenny, whom Adams called his wife, fled Pitcairn aboard a visiting ship in 1817. She recounted how, when the usual visitors crowded on board the *Bounty* during its final visit to Tahiti, Christian had ordered the anchor cable cut while they were below decks.

He first told the women that the ship was only going around the island, but once they passed through the reef, they realized he had lied. One even jumped overboard to try to swim to shore.

After that, Christian always kept the ship too far from land for other women to attempt to escape, although he did put ashore, on an island five or six leagues (a short distance) from Tahiti, six of the women who "were rather ancient."[11]

Once the *Bounty* had been burned, the women had no choice but to work for their survival and that of the men. "Passed around from one 'husband' to the other, as men died and the balance of power shifted, they rebelled," Alexander wrote.[12]

Edward Young, whose diary Beechey retrieved from Pitcairn Island, wrote that after the massacre, the women desperately wanted to build a boat and leave the island. Eventually, the men gave in, but the small boat—completed on August 13, 1794, and launched on August 15—capsized.

Shortly thereafter, according to John Adams, "a conspiracy of the women to kill the white men in their sleep was discovered."[13] The men decided among

© National Maritime Museum, Greenwich, London

**Thursday October Christian, son of Fletcher Christian. He greeted the British ships when they came upon the tiny island in 1808.**

# Reality vs. the Movie: The Pitcairn Women

Caroline Alexander makes a point of listing the names of the women taken to Pitcairn, who, she says, "made the Pitcairn experiment succeed" but have "rarely been evoked."[14]

They were Mauatua (Christian's wife), Vahineatua, Teio (and her small daughter, Teatuahitea), Faahotu, Teraura, Obuarei, Tevarua, Toofaiti, Mareva, Tinafornea, and Jenny (Teehuteatuaonoa).

In *The Bounty*, Mauatua is the beloved daughter of King Tynah, and Christian's love for her and desire to return to Tahiti to be with her is one of the primary reasons he leads the mutiny.

themselves that the first woman who misbehaved would be put to death, but this never happened.

After her escape from the island in 1817, Jenny finally returned to her home, arriving back in Tahiti thirty-one years after being taken from it.

## The Last Mutineer

Adams died in March 1829, one day after his sixty-sixth birthday. Some of his ever-changing accounts helped cement the notion that William Bligh was a tyrant who goaded his men into the mutiny.

Although Bligh was still alive when Pitcairn Island was rediscovered, he never commented publicly on the reports coming from it.

Pitcairn Island became a part of the British Empire. In 1831 its people were briefly relocated to Tahiti, but they soon returned. In 1856 overpopulation forced another relocation, this time to Norfolk Island, but five families made their way back to Pitcairn once more.

Today, descendants of the *Bounty* mutineers and their Tahitian wives still live on Pitcairn Island, where January 23 is celebrated every year as *Bounty* Day.

# Chapter 8

# The Movies

The drama inherent in the story of the mutiny on the *Bounty* has captivated people since Bligh first released his *Narrative*. When the new medium of film came along, it did not take long for someone to try to tell the story on the silver screen. The first film version, *The Mutiny on the Bounty*, was a black-and-white silent film released in Australia in 1916.

The next wave of movies was triggered by a best-selling trio of novels by Charles Nordhoff and James Norman Hall that appeared in 1932. The *Bounty Trilogy* comprised *Mutiny on the Bounty*, *Men Against the Sea*, and *Pitcairn Island*. The books told the story through a fictional first-person narrator called Roger Byam, based on Peter Heywood.

In 1933 an Australian film based on the *Bounty Trilogy* called *In the Wake of the Bounty* appeared, starring Errol Flynn as Fletcher Christian. It led to his being invited to Hollywood, where he became a major star.

### The 1935 and 1962 Versions

Two years later, MGM Studios remade *In the Wake of the Bounty* as *Mutiny on the Bounty*, directed by Frank Lloyd.

Shot on location in Tahiti, as well as on Catalina Island, in Santa Barbara, and in the MGM studios, the film went over budget, eventually costing about $2 million, but it was also the highest-grossing film of 1935, bringing in $4.5 million, and it won the Academy Award for Best Picture. Starring Clark Gable as Fletcher Christian and Charles Laughton as William Bligh, it was a great adventure film, but far from historically accurate.

> The drama inherent in the story of the mutiny on the *Bounty* has captivated people since Bligh first released his *Narrative*.

In this film version, Bligh is on board the *Pandora* when she sails to Tahiti, and he is present at the mutineers' court-martial. He is portrayed as an absolute villain, so cruel that it is clear he was entirely to blame for the mutiny. He is blamed for the death of the ship's doctor, who in real life drank himself to death.

A fourth version of the story, filmed in 1962, starred Marlon Brando as Fletcher Christian and Trevor Howard

Several movies based on the *Bounty* mutiny have been made. These were filmed in 1935 (top) and 1962.

as William Bligh. Again Bligh is portrayed as a vicious tyrant. Far from being friends before and during most of the voyage, as history indicates, Bligh and Christian are shown to hate each other from the beginning.

## The Bounty

In 1984 a new version of the story appeared that did not draw on the 1932 trilogy. Instead, *The Bounty* was based on Richard Hough's nonfiction book entitled *Captain Bligh and Mr. Christian*.

The original idea was to shoot two films simultaneously under the direction of David Lean. Lean worked on the project for several years with screenwriter Robert Bolt until the studio withdrew its support.

With Italian producer Dino De Laurentiis now providing funding, Roger Donaldson from New Zealand was brought in to direct. He only had a few months to prepare, but fortunately, the most important set piece had already been built: HMAV *Bounty* III, a same-size replica of the original ship. The ship was built in 1978 at a cost of $5 million.

After all those years, the film was shot in only eight weeks in three widely separated locations: London, Tahiti, and New Zealand. Vangelis, famous for his work on the movie *Chariots of Fire*, provided the evocative sound track.

## The Cast

Today it seems like the cast featured a remarkable number of stars. In 1984 they were not all as famous as they would later be.

The *Bounty* as she appears in the 1984 film. The movie closes with the burning of the ship by the mutineers.

Mel Gibson, then still a relative newcomer to Hollywood, played Fletcher Christian (Christopher Reeve turned down the role; Sting and David Essex were also considered). Anthony Hopkins played William Bligh. Laurence Olivier appeared in one of his final movie roles as Admiral Hood, presiding over Bligh's court-martial (though in real life Hood did not). Edward Fox played the skeptical Captain Moses Greetham.

Daniel Day-Lewis, in one of his first major screen appearances, played sailing master John Fryer, and Liam Neeson played the violent Charles Churchill.

Others in the cast included Bernard Hill as William Cole, Philip Davis as Edward Young, Wi Kuki Kaa as King Tynah, Tevaite Vernette as Mauatua, Philip Martin Brown as John Adams, Simon Chandler as David Nelson, and Malcolm Terris as the terminally drunk Dr. Huggan.

Many other actual crew members were also portrayed. Two who were not were Peter Heywood and Thomas Hayward. Instead, they were combined into a composite character named Thomas Heywood, played by Simon Adams. Since Hayward was one of the most loyal young officers and Peter Heywood remained with the mutineers, it was an odd choice. Perhaps the filmmakers did not want to confuse the audience with two characters with similar names.

## The Film

The film, structured as an extended flashback, begins with Bligh appearing before his court-martial for losing his ship and cuts back to his testimony periodically throughout. The movie ends with Blight's exoneration and the mutineers watching the *Bounty* burning off the shore of Pitcairn Island.

As highlighted in the boxes throughout this book, historically the film was reasonably, though not entirely, accurate. Certainly, for most of the film, Bligh is far more sympathetic than he had ever been portrayed before, although near the end the film, just before the mutiny occurs, he seems almost deranged.

Visually, the film is gorgeous, thanks to on-location shooting in and around Tahiti and New Zealand. The film is also notable in being the first film version in which the Tahitian women are portrayed topless, as historically they would have been.

## Mixed Reviews

Critical reaction was mixed. Critic Roger Ebert gave the movie his highest rating: four stars. He said Anthony Hopkins's performance made Bligh "unyielding, but not mindlessly rigid . . . completely loyal to his ideas of a British naval officer's proper duties."[1]

Gibson's Fletcher, Ebert wrote, "is a man of very few words . . . quiet, observant, an enigma. . . . It is a decision of some daring to give Gibson so noticeably little dialogue in this movie, but it works."[2]

Overall, Ebert called *The Bounty* "high-spirited and intelligent . . . a great adventure, a lush romance, and a good movie."[3]

At the other extreme, *Newsday*'s review of the movie consisted of only four words: "Man the bilge pumps."[4]

The review in *The New York Times* was longer, but not much more positive. "On the basis of three films" (the other two were *King Kong* and *Hurricane*), "it is

In *The Bounty*, Fletcher Christian was played by Mel Gibson (left), and William Bligh by Anthony Hopkins.

now possible to say that the Pacific Ocean is not Dino De Laurentiis's cup of tea," the review by Vincent Canby began.

Canby actually thought the film was too historically accurate. By making Bligh "a less mad character than we've known him to be in the earlier films, 'The Bounty' makes Fletcher Christian's behavior seem nothing more than petulant," Canby wrote.

"The movie seems to have been planned, written, acted, shot and edited by people who were constantly being overruled by other people. It's totally lifeless."[5]

The public seems to have agreed: The film was not a notable financial success.

The efforts that began shortly after the court-martial of the mutineers to portray Bligh as the villain of the mutiny worked in part because the romantic notion of the sensitive, tortured hero pushed by a tyrant into revolution is a classic template of storytelling.

In the realm of public perception, and in the realm of motion pictures, the more complicated and nuanced truth simply could not compete.

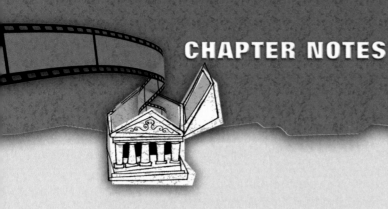

# CHAPTER NOTES

 **The Voyage of the *Bounty***

1. William Dampier, *A New Voyage Round the World* (London: Adam and Charles Black, 1937), <http://gutenberg.net.au/ebooks05/0500461h.html#ch 10> (January 17, 2008).

2. "Patronage and Promotion," *Broadside—Home of Nelson's Navy,* n.d., <http://www.nelsonsnavy.co.uk/ patronage.html> (January 18, 2007).

3. Caroline Alexander, *The Bounty* (New York: Penguin Group, 2005), p. 44.

4. Ibid., p. 46.

5. William Bligh and Edward Christian, *The Bounty Mutiny* (New York: Penguin Books, 2001), p. 198.

6. Richard Hough, *Captain Bligh and Mr. Christian: The Men and the Mutiny* (New York: E.P. Dutton & Co., Inc., 1973), p. 64.

7. Ibid., p. 67.

8. Alexander, p. 49.

9. "Patronage and Promotion."

10. Hough, pp. 54–55.

11. Alexander, p. 58.

12. Hough, p. 59.

13. Ibid., p. 60.

14. Alexander, p. 59.

15. Andrew Lambert, "Nelson's Navy: Life in the 18th-Century Royal Navy," n.d., <http://www.channel4.com/

history/microsites/H/history/n-s/nelson.html> (January 22, 2008).

16. Alexander, p. 84.

17. William Bligh, "Bounty Logbook, February 9, 1788," *Fateful Voyage*, August 1, 2008, <http://www.fateful voyage.com/logbook/log880201.html> (February 10, 2009).

18. Alexander, p. 85.

19. William Bligh, "Bounty Logbook, March 10, 1788," *Fateful Voyage*, August 3, 2008, <http://www.fateful voyage.com/logbook/log880302.html> (February 10, 2009).

20. William Bligh, "Bounty Logbook, May 24, 1788," *Fateful Voyage*, August 4, 2008, <http://www.fatefulvoyage. com/logbook/log880524.html> (February 10, 2009).

21. Alexander, p. 97.

22. James Morrison, "James Morrison's Journal," *Fateful Voyage*, May 31, 2008, <http://www.fatefulvoyage.com/ morrison/morrisonEMutiny.html> (February 10, 2009).

23. Ibid.

 **2 Tahiti**

1. William Bligh, "Bounty Logbook, October 26, 1788," *Fateful Voyage*, May 26, 2008, <http://www.fateful voyage.com/logbook/log881026.html> (February 10, 2009).

2. "Orders Issued by William Bligh Concerning the Conduct of the Men of the *Bounty*," *The* Bounty *Mutineers Trial Home Page*, n.d., <http://www.law .umkc.edu/faculty/projects/ftrials/Bounty/bligh logorders.html> (June 17, 2008).

3. William Bligh, "Bounty Logbook, December 29, 1788," *Fateful Voyage*, August 20, 2008, <http://www.fateful

voyage.com/logbook/log881229.html> (February 10, 2009).

4. William Bligh, "Bounty Logbook, January 5, 1789," *Fateful Voyage*, August 21, 2008, <http://www.fateful voyage.com/logbook/log890105.html> (February 10, 2009).

5. Caroline Alexander, *The Bounty* (New York: Penguin Group, 2005), pp. 117–118.

6. William Bligh, "Bounty Logbook, January 17, 1789," *Fateful Voyage*, August 21, 2008, <http://www.fateful voyage.com/logbook/log890116.html> (February 10, 2009).

7. Alexander, p. 118.

8. Richard Hough, *Captain Bligh and Mr. Christian: The Men and the Mutiny* (New York: E.P. Dutton & Co., Inc., 1973), pp. 125–126.

9. William Bligh, "Bounty Logbook, March 7, 1789," *Fateful Voyage*, August 29, 2008, <http://www.fateful voyage.com/logbook/log890302.html> (February 10, 2009).

 **The Mutiny**

1. William Bligh and Edward Christian, *The Bounty Mutiny* (New York: Penguin Books, 2001), p. 177.

2. John Fryer, "John Fryer's Narrative of the Mutiny," *Fateful Voyage*, May 24, 2008, <http://www.fateful voyage.com/fryer/fryerMutinyP01.html> (February 10, 2009).

3. William Bligh, "Bounty Logbook, April 24, 1789," *Fateful Voyage*, September 4, 2008, <http://www.fateful voyage.com/logbook/log890424.html> (February 10, 2009).

4. James Morrison, "James Morrison's Journal," *Fateful Voyage*, May 31, 2008, <http://www.fatefulvoyage.com/morrison/morrisonEMutiny.html> (February 10, 2009).

5. Fryer.

6. Ibid.

7. Morrison.

8. Bligh and Christian, p. 136.

9. Fryer.

10. Morrison.

11. Ibid.

12. Bligh and Christian, p. 137.

13. Richard Hough, *Captain Bligh and Mr. Christian: The Men and the Mutiny* (New York: E.P. Dutton & Co., Inc., 1973), p. 15.

14. Bligh and Christian, p. 8.

15. Caroline Alexander, *The Bounty* (New York: Penguin Group, 2005), p. 140.

16. Hough, p. 157.

17. Bligh and Christian, p. 10.

18. "Statement and Defense Witnesses for Thomas Burkett (9/17/1792)," *The* Bounty *Mutineers Trial Home Page*, n.d., <http://www.law.umkc.edu/faculty/projects/FTRIALS/Bounty/burketttranscript.html> (June 19, 2008).

## 4 Bligh's Voyage and Christian's Troubles

1. William Bligh, "Bounty Logbook, April 24, 1789," *Fateful Voyage*, August 22, 2008, <http://www.fatefulvoyage.com/logbook/log890124.html> (February 10, 2009).

2. William Bligh, "A Voyage to the South Sea," *Fateful Voyage*, May 30, 2008, <http://www.fatefulvoyage.com/bligh/blighVoyageCh14.html> (February 10, 2009).

3. Ibid.

4. Ibid.

5. William Bligh and Edward Christian, *The Bounty Mutiny* (New York: Penguin Books, 2001), p. 55.

6. William Bligh, "A Voyage to the South Sea," *Fateful Voyage*, May 30, 2008, <http://www.fatefulvoyage.com/bligh/blighVoyageCh17.html> (February 10, 2009).

7. Ibid.

8. Bligh and Christian, p. 145.

9. Richard Hough, *Captain Bligh and Mr. Christian: The Men and the Mutiny* (New York: E.P. Dutton & Co., Inc., 1973), p. 198.

10. Ibid., p. 200.

 ## 5  Arrests and Trial

1. Caroline Alexander, *The Bounty* (New York: Penguin Group, 2005), pp. 156–157.

2. Ibid., p. 159.

3. Ibid., p. 164.

4. Ibid., p. 186.

5. Peter Heywood, "Peter Heywood Letter to Mother from Batavia (1791)," *Fateful Voyage*, May 24, 2008, <http://www.fatefulvoyage.com/heywood/heywoodAMotherBatavia.html> (February 10, 2009).

6. Alexander, p. 202.

7. Ibid., p. 207.

8. "Articles of War," *Fateful Voyage*, January 17, 2009, <http://www.fatefulvoyage.com/misc/articles.html> (February 10, 2009).

 ## 6  The Testimony

1. "Testimony of William Purcell (9/13/1792)," *The Bounty Mutineers Trial Home Page*, n.d., <http://www.law

.umkc.edu/faculty/projects/ftrials/Bounty/purcell transcript.html> (June 19, 2008).

2. "Defense Witnesses for Peter Heywood and Statement by Peter Heywood (9/17/1792)," *The* Bounty *Mutineers Trial Home Page*, n.d., <http://www.law.umkc.edu/faculty/projects/ftrials/Bounty/heywoodtranscript.html> (June 19, 2008).

3. Ibid.

4. Ibid.

5. "Testimony of Lt. John Hallett (9/14/1792)," *The* Bounty *Mutineers Trial Home Page*, n.d., <http://www.law.umkc.edu/faculty/projects/ftrials/Bounty/hallett transcript.html> (June 19, 2008).

6. Ibid.

 **The Verdict and What Came After**

1. "Verdict and Sentence in the Court-Martial of the *Bounty* Mutineers," *The* Bounty *Mutineers Trial Home Page*, n.d., <http://www.law.umkc.edu/faculty/projects/ftrials/Bounty/verdict.html> (June 19, 2008).

2. Ibid., p. 300.

3. Peter Heywood, "Peter Heywood Letter to Edward Christian (1792)," *Fateful Voyage*, April 24, 2008, <http://www.fatefulvoyage.com/heywood/heywood HChristian.html> (February 10, 2009).

4. Caroline Alexander, *The Bounty* (New York: Penguin Group, 2005), pp. 325–332.

5. William Bligh and Edward Christian, *The Bounty Mutiny* (New York: Penguin Books, 2001), p. 176.

6. Ibid., p. 178.

7. Alexander, p. 337.

8. Bligh and Christian, p. 176.

9. Alexander, p. 397.

10. Ibid., p. 355.

11. Bligh and Christian, p. 230.
12. Alexander, p. 369.
13. Bligh and Christian, p. 251.
14. Alexander, p. 397.

 8   The Movies

1. Roger Ebert, "The *Bounty*," *Chicago Sun-Times*, January 1, 1984.
2. Ibid.
3. Ibid.
4. "Mutiny on the *Bounty*," *Solar Navigator*, 2006, <http://www.solarnavigator.net/mutiny_on_the_bounty.htm> (February 12, 2008).
5. Vincent Canby, "'The *Bounty*,' Capt. Bligh Story by Dino De Laurentiis," *The New York Times*, May 4, 1984.

# GLOSSARY

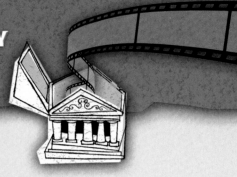

**able seaman**—The top class into which nonofficers were rated on a ship's books, a notch above ordinary seaman.

**Admiralty**—The division of the British government in charge of the Royal Navy's affairs.

**armorer**—The officer in charge of keeping small arms and swords in good repair and performing general metalworking.

**boatswain**—The officer in charge of boats, sails, rigging, anchors, cables, etc.

**bow**—The front end of a ship.

**carpenter**—The officer responsible for keeping a ship's frame, masts, and other wooden parts in good repair.

**court-martial**—A court composed of admirals, captains, and commanders that tries those accused of offenses under the Articles of War.

**cutlass**—A short, curving sword.

**cutter**—A small, single-masted sailboat.

**flagship**—The ship that carries the commander of a fleet and flies the commander's flag.

**flog**—To beat with a whip. A form of punishment in the Royal Navy.

**flotsam**—Floating wreckage from a ship or its cargo.

**fo'c'sle**—Short for forecastle. A short, raised deck at the very front of a ship.

**frigate**—A light, nimble warship that in Bligh's time carried between twenty and fifty guns.

**gangway**—A narrow platform that runs the length of the ship from the quarterdeck to the forecastle.

**grapeshot**—A collection of small shot bagged together and shot out of a cannon, designed to kill and maim rather than cause any great damage to another vessel.

**grapnel**—A small anchor.

**grog**—A mixture of rum and water.

**gunner**—The officer in charge of a ship's cannons and their powder and ammunition.

**launch**—A large, flat-bottomed boat that can be rowed or sailed.

**malaria**—A disease transmitted by mosquitoes that causes periodic attacks of chills and fever.

**master**—The officer, ranking just under the lieutenants, who is responsible for the navigation and sailing of a ship from port to port, under the direction of the captain.

**master's mate**—An officer who assists the master and ranks under him.

**midshipman**—A junior officer, or officer in training, usually still in his teens.

**port**—The left side of a ship as you face the bow.

**quartermaster**—An officer responsible for, among other things, stowing cargo, overseeing the steering, and keeping time.

**schooner**—A small sailing vessel with two masts.

**scurvy**—A disease caused by vitamin C deficiency. Symptoms include spongy gums, loose teeth, and bleeding into the skin and mucous membranes.

**squall**—A sudden, violent windstorm, often involving rain or snow.

**starboard**—The right side of the ship as you face the bow.

**stern**—The rear end of a ship.

**surgeon**—The medically trained officer responsible for treating any illness or injuries among the crew.

**yard**—A long piece of timber suspended from the mast of a ship, along which the sails are extended.

**yardarm**—The outer end of a yard.

**yawl**—A small rowboat.

Alexander, Caroline. *The Bounty.* New York: Penguin Group, 2005.

Barrow, Sir John. *Mutiny! The Real History of the H.M.S. Bounty*. New York: Cooper Square Press, 2003.

Bligh, William, adapted by Deborah Kestel. *The Mutiny on Board H.M.S. Bounty.* Edina, Minn.: ABDO Publishing, 2002.

Guttridge, Leonard F. *Mutiny: A History of Naval Insurrection.* New York: Berkley Books, 2002.

O'Brien, Patrick. *The Mutiny on the Bounty.* New York: Walker and Co., 2007.

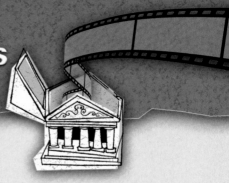

**Story of the Court-Martial of the *Bounty* Mutineers**
<http://www.law.umkc.edu/faculty/projects/ftrials/Bounty/bountyhome.html>

**The Historical Maritime Society: Nelson and His Navy**
<http://www.hms.org.uk/nelsonsnavymain.htm>

**Pitcairn Islands Study Center**
<http://library.puc.edu/pitcairn/>

# INDEX